Khuriyat Khudaymurodova

NATURE OF IMAGES IN NOVELS

© Khuriyat Khudaymurodova
Nature of Images in Novels
by: Khuriyat Khudaymurodova
Edition: October '2024
Publisher:
Taemeer Publications LLC (Michigan, USA / Hyderabad, India)

ISBN 978-93-5872-946-7

© **Khuriyat Khudaymurodova**

Book	:	**Nature of Images in Novels**
Author	:	Khuriyat Khudaymurodova
Publisher	:	Taemeer Publications
Year	:	'2024
Pages	:	130
Title Design	:	*Taemeer Web Design*

This monograph is based on Khuriyat Khudoymurodova's dissertation on "Artistic skill of Nadir Normatov" written for the degree of doctor of philosophy (PhD) in philology. The book is intended for students studying in the field of philology, researchers, literary critics, and a wide audience of readers interested in literature.

Responsible Editor:

Ulugbek Hamdamov doctor of philological sciences

Reviewers:

Normat Yoldoshev

Candidate of philological sciences, associate professor

Gulnoza Jo'rakulova

Candidate of Philosophy (PhD), associate professor

INTRODUCTION

In world literature, a number of studies have been created about the creative process and the integrity of artistic skill, the basis of its realization in the work, its individuality in the use of its own language, form and visual means. It's no secret that art does not have a single criterion and dimensions, patterns. In the science of literature, there are a number of scientific-theoretical approaches to the criteria of artistry. In general, each artist has his own artistic universe.

The need to reflect the biographical information of the creator in his work, to identify the factors manifested in the individual style, to show that the style is a unique poetic category, to research a number of problems such as the image, the language of the work as a whole system has always been urgent. During the years of independence, many achievements were made in the field of research of fiction from the point of view of creative-individual style in our country. In current Uzbek literary studies, the analysis of the artistic work and the illumination of the poetic skill of the creator are approached on the basis of various research methods of world literary studies. A monographic study of the creative heritage of the well-known representative of Uzbek literature, Nodir Normatov, the unique qualities of his works, and the artistic skills of the writer are among the important tasks of literary studies.

A number of articles and reviews of Nodir Normatov's works have been published. N. Khudoyberganov, U. Normatov, I. Gafurov, A. Ulug'ov, I. Yaqubov, Sh. Davronova, S. Tolaganova expressed their opinion about the work of the writer in our literary studies. In the dissertations of I. Yaqubov and F. Khadjaeva, the works of Nodir Normatov served as a source to some extent for studying the issues. In Khuriyat Khudoymurodova's dissertation entitled "Artistic skills of Nodir Normatov", the writer's laboratory was studied in a separate monographic plan. We hope that the scientific views and conclusions reflected in our research will help to assess the issues of artistic skill of Nodir Normatov.

The nature of images in the novel "The Two in the Mirror"

The literary generation of the 70s and 80s stands out in Uzbek literature. Literary critics and literary experts especially recognize the creativity of representatives of this generation: "The social mood associated with the collapse of faith in the idea and the feeling of the need for fundamental social changes (including independence) determined the ideological and aesthetic position of the generation of the 70s." Indeed, in the literature of this period, the erosion of the politics of the existing system began to show. At first glance, the emergence of the creativity of representatives of this period is natural and reasonable.

It is known that in the literature of the 60s and 70s, works reflecting the life of young people increased. The "heroism" of young people on the way to the implementation of former socialist ideas was reflected. During this period, the image of young people and their place in society became a leading issue in the works of most of our writers, such as Odil Yakubov, Pirimkul Kadyrov, Olmas Umarbekov, O'tkir Hoshimov, Shukur Kholmirzaev. Including "Yaira wants to enter the institute", "Erk", "Kadrim", "Peers", "Wings will be paired", "Crystal chandeliers", "Two springs of Damir Usmanov", "My love, my beloved", "Summer rain", " Who is not eighteen?" Dozens of works like

In the late 1970s and early 1980s, the "era of transparency" appeared in the society. These changes were more profound in fiction. In the created works, we come across images with a new way of thinking. These new types of images are first of all inextricably linked with the artistic reflection of the socio-aesthetic views of the creators who are their authors.

Writers such as M.M.Dost, T.Murod, Kh.Sultanov, E.Azam, N.Normat, who were called the literary generation of the 70s and 80s, brought a new tone and charm to literature. The works of M.M.Dost and E.A'zam differ from each other with the sarcasm in relation to reality, the friendly style rich in national melodies in the work of T.Murod, and the primacy of the lyrical spirit in the works of H.Sultan. Among these prose writers, Nadir Normatov's work is distinguished by its style and tone. The wide possibilities and variety of realism are evident in the work of the writer. In his work, the forms of artistic conventionality of folk art, elements of magical realism can be felt. N. Normatov's artistic representation of the realities of life is based on reality, i.e. documentary. The writer himself emphasizes this: the process of writing the story "Uncle Ismail's Scales" was complicated. Documentary has limited me. In the story "The Punishment" I am also based on documents. But I am creative with the available evidence. In general, I rely on documentary in almost all my works." This is evident when observing the author's work.

First, let's think about the writer's life path, the environment in which he was born and raised.

Nadir Normatov was born on December 24, 1950 in the village of Poshkhurd, Sherabad district, Surkhandarya region. -Hills rich in various herbs, sometimes gushing, sometimes trickling streams, hidden and open brooks passing through the courtyards, stone walls, thorn and rose flowers, narrow streets and broad-hearted people, their joyful noises are in my heart. As the poet said, "I am everywhere, my heart is with you." Every time I came to the village, it seemed to me that it had not changed for many years, although something had changed, I did not want to admit it, I kept putting it in the unknown, the unseen. But when I came this year, in the spring, I noticed that it had changed a lot, and it was no longer the Poshkhurd that I left forty-seven years ago. I don't just mean its views, its scenery. The appearance, behavior, and character of the people living here, including their unfamiliarity, reminded me at every step that it had changed. It made my heart rumble. It is true that all the villagers here, both familiar and unfamiliar, show me respect, respect is in order. But that's not the point. For some reason, I feel like a stranger here. No matter what I do, the world is always changing, you have to get used to it. But the ancient Dabilkurgan fortress, which is dear to me, the old cemetery where the remains of my ancestors are buried, Poshkhurdsay, where I spent my childhood, the hills and gorges in the Oktogu Karatog valley have not changed in my mind. It seems like a good news. Maybe it's the ghost of a memory that's stuck in my mind. But still, they are immutable to me. For some reason, when I was writing these words, I had tears in my eyes, maybe these tears came from inside my heart to tell them."

The writer writes in his biography: "My father Normat Alimardonov was an accountant by profession. Even when he slept, his hand was shaking. Sidqidildan worked in this field for more than fifty years. At the same time, he was a very well-read, literate, lazy person. The years of the beginning of writing - in 1970, the war caused disability and he retired early. He died in 1991 at the age of 67. My father was one of the people I knew who looked forward to independence the most. Because his father Alimardon was imprisoned (in 1937) as a blue-collar worker and died in one of the prisons of Termiz, and he was one of those who experienced the tragedy of those years. My mother Bobalova (actually Bobalieva) was a Kyzlaroy teacher, who died very early - at the age of 31, in 1958, when I was eight years old. I think my mother was a good teacher, because when I was three or four years old I learned to carve my name on the walls of the house with a knife.

I graduated from school in the village with a silver medal. During my school days, I participated in district and regional Olympiads in various subjects. In 1966, I took 2nd place at the poetry conference organized by the regional youth committee. I started my work by drawing poems and pictures, writing articles. I don't remember exactly which one I started first, I think it must have been from the picture. However, I remember that my first poems and pictures were dedicated to the Kohitang mountains, which surround the village and appear black and white from afar, and are called Oktog and Karatog among the local people. One of my poems was published in "Yangiabad" newspaper of Sherabad district when I was in the 5th grade.

Mamaraim Boykulov, his villager, close confidant, well-known pedagogue, remembers Adib's childhood years and his entry into creativity: "After the death of Nadir's mother, mourners joined the ranks of guests who often came to the house. Now Nadir's anxiety has increased, he has no time for rest or lessons. Moreover, the fairy-tale books, "Little Red Riding Hood" and "Bogursok", which his mother read to him and which he later memorized independently, did not meet his needs. Among the rare ones, our winter yard contained a collective farm office, a one-room library, a summer club, a grain storehouse, a barber shop, and it was a kind of picnic area. Nadir often passed through these lands and came to the village library. I clearly remember that the books there were Nadir's main interlocutor and helped him to forget his worries and to get rid of his mother's grief a little. He spent his free time passing through the roof of the house where he lived with his mother, and started reading books in the attic of the new house. Now he took "Uzbek Folk Tales", "Russian Folk Tales", poetry books from the village library and organized a secret library in the attic. An old blanket left by his mother, a pillow, wooden boxes empty of soap were the equipment of his studio. Nadir began to practice poems here. At first, poetic exercises appeared on sheets, in small notebooks, and later in thick notebooks.

I remember the content of some poems he wrote as a child. For example, in the poem "Dog'" he wrote about the bad thing about the stain, saying that "if a stain appears on your face, a little baby will be born", he described the good quality of the stain. Don't such lines mean how observant, how fluent the thoughts of a young teenager are, how boldly he looks at life?!" Observation of life, deep observation can also be felt from the first creative exercises of the future writer.

Adib studied at the Faculty of Journalism of Tashkent State University in 1967-72. In the year he graduated from the university, his research "Image of our contemporary in documentaries" was published consecutively in the 1972 editions of the "Uzbekistan culture" newspaper. In 1972-74, he was an assistant director, editor, editor-in-chief of the slide film department at the scientific-popular and documentary film studio of Uzbekistan, in 1974-79, at the invitation of the

People's Poet of Uzbekistan Zulfia, he was the department head in the magazine "Saodat", in 1979-83 he was the department head in the magazine "Soviet Uzbekistan". head, in 1983 he was the head of the department at the "Literature and Art of Uzbekistan" week, which was edited by the national writer of Uzbekistan Odil Yaqubov, in 1983-1988 he worked as a freelance artist, in 1989-91 he worked as a chief specialist, head of the department, deputy chairman of the Culture Fund of Uzbekistan. In 1992-1997, he was a chief specialist, head of department at the Ministry of Cultural Affairs of Uzbekistan. Since 1997, chief specialist at the Academy of Arts of Uzbekistan, commercial director at the International Relations Center. Since 1998, he has been the deputy editor-in-chief of the "San'at" magazine, which is published in three languages - Uzbek, Russian, and English, and since 2000, he has been the editor-in-chief. Since 2009, he has been working as the head of the Information and International Relations Department of the Academy of Arts of Uzbekistan. Nadir Normatov, along with being the head of the department, also carried out pedagogical activities. In 2008-2009, he taught the science of editing and review to master's and bachelor's students of the National Institute of Painting and Design named after Kamoliddin Behzod.

Nadir Normatov became known as a talented writer and art critic in the early 1970s. His first story - "Tiniqgul" was published in 1974 in "Saodat" magazine. In 1977, the first book entitled "Kohitang stories" was published (Adabiyot va sanat publishing house named after G. Ghulam). The second collection of stories and short stories "Birds flew from the cliff" was published in 1986. "Owner of holy fish" (1981, "Yosh Leninchi" newspaper), "Man under the tree" (1988, "Yoshlik" magazine), "Bisot" (1982, "Yoshlik" magazine, issue 6), "Ismail "Uncle's scales" (1987, "Yoshlik" magazine, No. 1), short stories "Jazo" (1985, "Yoshlik" magazine, No. 6), novel "Barigal" (1991, "Kamalak" publishing house) . In these works, the lifestyle and thoughts of rural people are described in a simple and impressive manner. The writer shows the character traits of his characters in clear symbols. Brightly embodies natural scenes. In the short story "The Man Under the Tree" and in the novel "Barigal" he tries to give a broader artistic interpretation of the inner world of man. Famous literary critic Ibrahim Gafurov wrote about this: "His first short story "Bisot" in 1981 and his novel "Barigal" published in 1991 caught the attention of the writer Said Ahmed. He welcomed teacher Nadir Normatov. In this novel, Nadir Normatov tried to find a new letter in prose, in which figurativeness and reality seem to be mixed. Nature is more open than any of us, more mysterious, more mysterious, wiser than any of us. Nadir achieves one thing without a doubt: he portrays natural people in a natural way and carves out human destinies and characters with the precise action of a mountain forester's ax. That's why the characters he drew, the events that shaped them, the environment, and the scenes of the conditions are extremely vivid and vivid. Qabil is a warrior in the story "Bisot", laboratory assistant, teacher Esonboy in the story "The Man Under the Tree", zoology teacher O'tamurod in the story "Owner of the Holy Fish", Mayram in "The Punishment", Raimboy and Qudratov in "Uncle Ismail's Scales", Mamatmirzo in "Summer Thunder". , the wonderful old woman in the story "Kar Momo" - these and the people around them are very natural and open, bubbly people. Their mistakes, nobleness, tragedies, dramas are also bubbles, Nadir Normatov does not try to decorate them and make them beautiful. He draws natural phenomena by finding their natural status. That's all. The word "drawing" perfectly matches the artistic method of Nodir Normatov, and formally characterizes this method. He likes to draw more than a detailed long shot, because there's a draw in a draw – Nadir draws the edges of a character with cross-hatching. From the events, the events are born at such intersecting points and connect with each other. Naturally, there is a risk of disorganization in the narrative, it is possible that the beginning, continuation and end of the story will not be connected. But the writer achieves wholeness and wholeness in the plot and composition by using some of his own narrative reserves without letting us know. The wholeness achieved in the style of a story by means of cross-cutting is a unique and visible edge of Nadir's writing skills and artistic style, which distinguishes him from others. So, is it possible to call it a natural style? That is, the manner of writing life and nature as it is. What is the natural way of life, which has been the priority for thousands of years, in the ancient villages between Muzrabot steppes, Kohitang mountains, Poshkhurd, Zarabog, and Vandob mountains. As a scientist who wrote many articles and book reviews about I. Gafurov's literary work, N. Normatov clearly and succinctly expresses the world of art.

Nadir Normatov has published hundreds of articles about the work of representatives of the world and Uzbek visual arts. The novel-essay "Rozi Choriev's last will" dedicated to the life and work of Musavvir Rozi Choriev was highly appreciated by art critics and the literary community and was translated into Russian. The book "House where the rainbow lives" was published for children about the artist. They describe the features and secrets of the art of painting.

Nadir Normatov's short stories, "Silver Nuts", "Punishment", "Uncle Ismail's Scales" were translated into Russian by the writer Ganna Nemirko from St. Petersburg (Leningrad) and "Golubye Orekhi" published under In cooperation with A. Madrahimov, he compiled and published the large collection "Schools of Eastern Miniatures", wrote the foreword.

Nodir Normatov is the author of the multimedia texts "Learning Shapes and Colors" (2008) created for young children.

At the same time, Nadir Normatov is the author of more than twenty documentaries about the figures of fine and applied arts, folk masters. His documentaries created during independence: "Miracle of Omonkhona", "Behzod Varislari", "Beshik" show another side of him. In addition, the writer's "Malik Nabiev", "Chingiz Akhmarov", "Golden foundations of Poshkhurd", "Langar", "Surkhan pottery", "Usta Abdugani", "Boisun's Gauguin", "Surkhan's bakhshi", "Kohitang mountain miracle", " So'zana", "Architectural Monuments Named after Women", "Sculptor Azamat", "Ceramic Tales of Kubaro Boboeva", "Rainbow or Remembering Rozi Choriev" (as Chief Advisor), 2010 "Stonemasons of Gozgon", "Sozanalari of Bukhara", "Sculptor " is the scriptwriter of documentaries.

N. Normatov is also a significant creator in the field of artistic photography. His works "Ko'hitang", "Khomkon", "Etyud prada", "Hashar", "Kichik Oshpaz" were exhibited in republican exhibitions. In 2007, the work "Little Chef" took 3rd place in the competition "Homeland Starts from the Neighborhood".

In December 2010, his personal art photo exhibition called "The Road to the Village" was successfully shown at the Tashkent Photo House.

N. Normatov is also a significant creator in the field of artistic photography. His works "Ko'hitang", "Khomkon", "Etyud prada", "Hashar", "Kichik Oshpaz" were exhibited in republican exhibitions. In 2007, the work "Little Chef" took 3rd place in the competition "Homeland Starts from the Neighborhood".

In December 2010, his personal art photo exhibition called "The Road to the Village" was successfully shown at the Tashkent Photo House.

Nodir Normatov has edited hundreds of books in the field of culture, art and publishing, and works in the field of artistic translation. He published the book "Pandnoma" from ancient Syrian monuments (in collaboration with G. Normatova), Russian writer K. He translated the short story "Isaac Levitan" by Paustovsky, the poem "Lomakon" by the Turkish writer Aziz Nesin, the short stories "Madina amma ertaklari" by the Azerbaijani writer Akram Aylisli (in collaboration with G. Normatova), the poems of Alexander Volkov, Yevgeny Melnikov, Rafael Toktash, and examples of Estonian poetry. The radio productions written by N. Normatov called "One day there was an ant" and "The man who chased the rainbow" were included in the golden fund of Uzteleradio.

In 2006, N. Normatov created the ceremonial anthem of the Academy of Arts of Uzbekistan in cooperation with the composer Rustam Abdullaev. In addition to working at the Academy of Arts, Nadir Normatov was engaged in public work. He participated as a jury member in various competitions. For several years, he gave lectures on art called "Colors, Tones, People" in different regions of Uzbekistan. He took an active part in the preparation of publications, books and albums on visual arts, published by the Academy of Arts of Uzbekistan, and in creative events. He took an active part in a series of shows and broadcasts on the visual and applied arts of Uzbekistan on television and radio.

In 2010, the writer was awarded the Order of "Labor Fame" for his artistic achievements. Nadir Normatov died in 2017.

If we look at the press of the 70s and 80s, we can see that the works of the authors of this period caused a lot of discussions, debates and debates by literary critics and literary critics. The work of Nadir Normatov did not escape their attention.

Critic Norboy Khudoyberganov in his article "Description alone is not enough" gives a reasoned opinion about the writer's short story "The Punishment". Regarding this story, which caused controversy in his time, the critic writes: In "Jazo" he (N. Normatov - H.K.) achieved such that in some places the characters are embodied before our eyes like living people: "Today, despite the fact that Mayram came back from work, his mouth was in his ear. He praised Mother Mergan, who came and went in and out of the house. He said that there is no equal to you in carpet making, he said that you are my mother instead of my mother, he repeatedly kissed her face and eyes and said that you are an excellent fortune teller. The old woman also got wet."

You can see that two women are enjoying themselves. After all, one - Mayram, a foreman at the horticulture state farm, was unable to pick the apples he had grown, and the other - Mergan Momo, as a veteran of the revolution, went to Raykom and organized the collection of those apples. is limited to itself, does not care about the in-depth coverage of the characteristics of both heroes as unique characters. From the beginning to the end of the story, both women are showered with slanderous praises, and they are busy reporting on who they met and what they did. And no matter how truthful and meaningful the information is, it is unable to show the image of the heroes, their inner world, and their unique human characteristics. In this respect, the critic is right. In the story, the writer used praise or criticism to show his positive and negative characteristics.

Literary experts and critics reacted to the author's work even when his first works were published. Even after the years of independence, the writer actively created. He worked not only as a writer, but also as an art critic and photographer. That's probably why the writer could not engage in literary creation later. But luck took each of them. In the following years, his new stories, the novel-essay "The Last Testament of Rozi Choriev" and the novel "The Tree of Zulayho" were published.

In 2008, Nadir Normatov's novel-essay "Rozi Choriev's last will" was published, in 2012 the collection of short stories and short stories "Bisot" and in 2013 the novel "Two in the Mirror" were published. A number of reviews and studies were created by literary experts about these works. In particular, Umarali Normatov published an article entitled "Impression of two stories" devoted to the analysis of the writer's stories "One day there was an ant..." and "The patterned flowers of the street door". The author looks at the artistic world of Nadir Normatov through the analysis of these two stories.

Ibrahim Gafurov wrote the foreword to the writer's selection "Bisot" and the novel

"Kozgudagi ikovlon". The leitmotif of the author's work is revealed in "Nadir's moonstone or the soul of Surkhan" written as a foreword to the "Bisot" selection: "The heroes of Nadir live in the embrace of nature, they certainly look for miracles from it, they believe in miracles wholeheartedly. Mysterious fish, fascinating blue nuts, blue stones, three hundred to five hundred-year-old trees, hundred-thousand-year-old ants and birds entering the language, attempts to reveal the charms of the universe and ancient life in magical conversations with people - these are also their charming solutions and tones in the natural artistic language of Nadir. has an accent."

In fact, if you look at the work of Nadir Normatov, it reflects the relationship between man and nature, the mysteries of the whole existence, and miracles beyond human progress. In fact, isn't the main task of literature to convey to the reader the artistic image and imagery, the relations of reality in them, the worldview and the processes of acceptance of the artistic work? Although the "main pressure" of Nadir Normatov's work is focused on nature and its mystery, the main character is, in fact, a human figure. True, there are some works in which the image of a person is not created. But, in fact, they also figuratively talk about human life, feelings, and destiny. Remember: Nodar Dumbadze's "Bronze Pig", Turgenov's "Mumu", Said Ahmed's

"Korakoz Majnun", Chingiz Aitmatov's "Farewell, Gulsari", Turob To'lan's "Don'an" are the focus of animals, but in fact they are humanized (thinks like a human, laughs, cries). He makes friends with people, does good, can show his feelings. Abdulla Ulugov's research occupies a special place in the study of Nadir Normatov's work. This collection includes his studies "Spiritual Ointment or Poison" and "Do You Know the Zulayha Tree or the Self-Searching Man?" The stories and stories included in N. Normatov's collection "Bisot" are analyzed in the larger "Spiritual ointment or poison". The author pays special attention to such issues as the general landscape of N. Normatov's work, the skill of artistic reflection of the relationship between man and nature, literary style, and aesthetic views. The main aspects of the writer's work are reflected in these comments of the researcher: "Nadir Normatov writes down the events he saw, observed, and was influenced by, and without getting caught up in small details, he focuses on the most important details of the time and place where the events took place. Being able to find the most important aspects in drawing the landscape of time and space means that the artist has clearly felt the essence of reality, the situation and experience of the characters. Nodir Normatov's short stories have the same feature. In his works, he expresses reality as he sees it. Therefore, the same scene comes to life in the imagination of the student." These studies of A. Ulug'ov are more descriptive-analytical in nature. It gives the impression that there is a lack of deep scientific and theoretical views. There is no doubt that there are valid and controversial points in all of these analyzes. Because the total existence of form and content in an artistic work, as well as the lack of uniformity in the classification of the components of form and content, fully characterize the "character" of this research. can justify.

We can see that the articles included in the collection reflect different aspects of the artistic world of Nodir Normatov. Sanobar Tolaganova connects the artistic expression typical of the writer's work to SOG'INCH. For example, "Nadir Normatov tries to show the artistic expression of SOGINCH in Uzbek prose through lines. His characters speak to each other with words that even the people of Surkhan oasis have forgotten."

In the article "Metamorphosis Motif in Contemporary Uzbek Prose", M. Kochkarova uses N. Normatov's story "Once an ant..." as a source. While researching this story in a comparative aspect, the author of the article makes a brief excursion into the genesis of the metamorphosis motif, which is the basis of the story. M. Kochkarova compares the story "One day there was an ant..." with the stories "The House in the Eyeball" by H. Dostmuhammad, "The Dog of Bahauddin" by N. Eshonqul and "Kismat" by I. Sultan. In general, the writer's story "Once upon a time there was an ant..." has caused the most debates in our literary studies. Researcher Sh.Davronova, while researching this story, compares it with the story of "Sulayman and Karinchka" from Rabguzi's "Kissai Rabguzi". In the studies of M. Kochkarova and Sh. Davronova, N. Normatov's story "One day there was an ant" is studied from different angles. New considerations and hypotheses about the story can be seen in them. The story is researched in the context of world literature and conclusions are drawn. The modernist, innovative spirit was able to reveal the essence of the story "Once upon a time there was an ant". Because another important element of creativity is imagination. After all, N. Normatov's story "Once upon a time there was an ant" is distinguished by its abundance of miracles, various life situations and various destinies, and characters with unique characters.

"Nadir Normatov" is a collection of articles and interviews about the writer's work published in the press after his death. The collection "His life and work in the eyes of his contemporaries" was published. In it, we can see a number of studies devoted to the analysis of the author's creativity and works. These studies play an important role in revealing certain aspects of the writer's creative world and artistic skills. These works serve as a special impetus and key to the detailed study of the author's work.

All of Nadir Normatov's stories included in the series "My stone epics" are autobiographical in nature. The writer artistically expresses the events he saw, knew, and experienced. Sometimes his childhood memories served as a motive.

If you read Nadir Normatov's stories from the series "My stone epics", you will witness that a stone is not just a simple, lifeless object, but some kind of divine power of nature is hidden in it.

In the story "Tashkoriz", the writer describes his memories of his father. The writer does not exaggerate reality in the story. Although his own father is at the center of the story, it does not shy away from reality. Haqqani shows the portrait of his father: "Although my father was not a cruel person, he was a strict and quick-tempered person. Every time my father got angry, my mother, who was spinning the yarn (she would never let go of her yarn, even if she went to the neighbor's house, she would be with him), cursed the war for some reason. It is understood that the cause of this anger in the Father is the war. We seem to understand the reason for such changes in the mentality of the father, who was thrown into the front lines of the war and faced death every time, because he was the son of Kulak. Although the war was over, his pain and wound did not heal. He changed the fate and dreams of a large generation. The war created a mood of despair in the psyche of the people.

Let's take a look at the next footage: "Mom says that father didn't drink before the war or during the war. My mother died when I was a little over eight years old, when the process of taking people from the village to the back of the mountain - to pick cotton - began. After that, our father became a frequent drinker. Especially after becoming the chief accountant at the collective farm, this situation escalated under the pretext of visiting guests."

The misfortune that befell the family caused the father to turn to alcohol. He gets all his pains from alcohol. He seeks "salvation" from it, relieves his heart from suffering for a while. In the story, this "characteristic" of the father is connected with the stone. We know that Koriz is a Persian word that means a complex water structure dug to bring underground water to the surface, a well from which water flows out [O'TIL-5, 2, 408]. The author tells the stonemason that they throw all the empty bottles into the stonemason, and their work is lightened. Once upon a time, rushing waters flowed from it, and the inhabitants enjoyed it. When the time of the Soviets came, the koriz was neglected, it was

turned into a dumping ground, it is expressed through the story of the mother:
"... Only the stone quarry here survived. But during that time, the red soldiers threw away our Arabic books, the pilgrims threw away their garbage, and buried their water. Here's the rest... ". It is known from history that during the Soviet era, our national values and traditions were violated, and holy places were destroyed. As if this was not enough, the holy springs and korizi were buried, turned into trash and garbage dumps. We know that spitting in water is also a sin. This tradition is still preserved today. This tradition, passed down from our ancestors, disappeared during the Soviet era. The writer's goal in this story is not simply to describe reality, to express childhood memories, but to reflect the bitter truth of the time. Tashkoriz, in fact, acted as a symbolic symbol of the entire era, taking in its filth, pains, and sorrows, and being a silent witness to it. Through the events that took place in his life, which he witnessed, the writer shows all the truths of the era of the authoritarian system, the mentality of the people. Even in scenes related to his father, he does not shy away from the truth. When you read the story "Tashkoriz", you will see the darkest days of the era with his own eyes, the father who faced death at every step in the war, lost his life partner, and his pain and

suffering. it gives the impression of burying one's dreams.

The story "Saifi Aka" was also written based on the writer's childhood memories. The author begins the story by saying, "There were a lot of noises and events related to stones in my childhood." Brother Saifi, who left the boy (writer) out of his car on his way to a wedding, was "pelted" with a stone by him. The most important thing is that soon after that, Saifi's brother fell seriously ill. He knows that he will get sick because he hurt the child and gives him a gift to wash away his "guilt". After this incident, Sayficha's character changes: "Well, Sayficha's wife said that after the stone of this child, that is, the stone I threw, her husband became a lover of children. People did not immediately believe in the truth of this statement. But in the meantime, an incident happened, and it turned out that Saificha really became a different person. One winter day, a neighbor's child fell seriously ill. At that time, there was no great doctor among the mountains. There would only be a paramedic. It is a long way to the center of the district, the roads at that time were steep and uneven, unpaved, thirty miles could be covered in five hours by car. In such a situation, the doctor is promised and brought big gifts from the center. Then, when he gave the gift himself, the doctor, when he found out about the incident, confessed to Sayficha and left without taking a penny. Sayficha's reputation has increased again.

On the face of it, Brother Saifi did a humanitarian job that any other person could have done. The fact that he became a different person because of a single stone is the main essence of the story. Here it is shown that the stone caused a change in human nature and character. Let's say that the main detail in the story is a stone, and the essence of it seems to be tied to it. In fact, the content of the work is related to this stone.

In the "Panji" story, the story about the stone served as the basis. The reality is given on the basis of childhood memories: "I remember with gratitude that the stone instilled in me, a child like me, a feeling of compassion and remorse. I remember that day like it was yesterday: we, ten-eleven-year-old boys, bathed in the stream near the mill on a summer day, sunbathed, and rode a horse made of willow twigs. We stopped when we came across the yard of Radiouzel. This place used to be the yard of the biggest rich man in Poshkhurd, and it was very neglected, now there was a big road running through the middle of the yard, and on one side there was a radio station, and on the other side there was a broken roof of the old sais house. We used to play on these roofs. I turned in that direction when a guy named Panji came out. I don't remember if he yelled at us or chased us, I took a stone from the ground and threw it at him. I can see that the stone hit him on the head. I saw that his head was cracked and bleeding, and I felt strange. If I still remember, why did I cut off the head of this innocent wretch? Panji the fool walked around with a gauze cloth on his head for several days. If he saw me, he would point to the people around him and insist that he hit me like this. This was my first regret, my first mistake, and this stone made me realize it" (Emphasis ours - H.K.).

But Panji later helps the boy when he falls into a ravine with his bicycle and loses consciousness, and most importantly, he does not reveal this "secret" to anyone. This reality awakens a lifelong debt and guilt in the writer to Panji. Even though Panji is a fool, he doesn't hurt anyone. He is a simple person who can tell the truth to people's faces. Panji is the face of the stupid village. Although he is crazy, he is truthful, simple, and most importantly, sincere.

In the above stories "Saifi Aka" and "Panji" the idea that the stone has a miraculous power capable of changing human nature is expressed. It is known that the stone is a hard rock. In our people, the expressions "stone-like metin" and "stone-like will" are used. Usually, the quality of "Baghritosh" is given to hard-tempered, unkind people. In the above stories, it is described that the same stone changed people of "good-natured" character for the better, which also shows another mystery of the universe and man. Shoira Doniyorova writes: "In both works ("Sayfi aka" and "Panji" - H.K.) the vices and virtues of human nature are expressed in connection with different views of the people through the stone detail and depicted in harmony with the imagination of the writer."

The author's stories "Saifi Aka" and "Panji" are more descriptive than descriptive. As if the work has no end, no knot. Is the writer's goal to show the changeability of human character, or to instill in the spirit of the work that the detail in the story is a tool? But the reality in them is not a product of the writer's fantasy, as Sh. Doniyorova pointed out. These stories are a reflection of the events that the writer himself saw and participated in directly. We know that a work of art is a system as a whole. A system is understood as a whole consisting of relations and communication. The essence of the elements of the system in the stories of N. Normatov "Sayfi aka" and "Panji" was manifested in the entire composition. We want to say that the narrative in these two stories was able to show the weak appearance of the biographical method.

The stories "Ashiqtash or American Stone in Love" and "Oytosh" are based on the writer's experiences during his trip to America. In a word, both stories can be called a travelogue.

In the story "Ashiqtash or an American Stone in Love", the author tells an interesting story about Zakir, an immigrant living in America, uncle of his son-in-law. In the work, the author describes the portrait of Aka Zakir as follows: "Aka Zakir is a strong, handsome man with a short beard, a turban on his head, a warm heart, and smiling eyes. I thought he was in his sixties, but he was a lively man who was approaching his seventies.
During the trip, the author observes Zakir brother. The storyteller is interested in the fact that girls and women always look at an object in their hands when they pass by: "When Zakir Aka looked at the women standing a little way from us and opened his palm again, I saw this scene while coming down the stairs. A stone like an egg with triangular inscriptions was lying in the palm of Aka Zakir.
Brother Zakir's faith in a simple stone shows his simplicity. He believes there is magic in a simple stone sold by another expatriate as a means of quickly seducing women. Believing in the magic of a simple stone, brother Zakir, who has spent a good amount of money, does not suffer from this work, he keeps waving his hand.
True, in this story, like in the stories of "Saifi Aka" or "Panji", the stone does not show any benefit. Maybe it just acts as a simple item. During the trip, the author discovers the simple, sincere, trusting brother Zakir.

The story "Oytosh" also describes what the author saw and experienced during his trip to America. The basis of the story is the writer's experiences and memories, who once saw a picture of a rock taken from the moon in a magazine and, as fate would have it, held it in his hand in the "Metropolitan" museum.

American astronaut Armstrong brought a sample of soil and rock from the lunar surface and it was published in a journal. As a child, Adib sees a picture of a moonstone in this magazine. The dream of seeing this moonstone is hidden in the heart of the writer. As fate would have it, N. Normatov, who traveled to the USA for an international conference with the poet Khurshid Davron, will take the magazine with him. He sees the moonstone kept in the "Metropolitan" museum. The author describes his feelings at this time as follows: "At this moment, we were sitting in a row, taking turns sitting in a special place, and I saw that moonstone placed on an elegant mirror. Everyone who was watching touched his palm, and the moonstone was polished from the palm of the hand and became shiny. I trembled with excitement. After all, not everyone is lucky enough to see this stone brought from the moon, from such a distance, and touch it with their hands. It is a difficult event for a child like me who once grew up in a village in the middle of a distant mountain on the Asian continent to go to the American continent and see the moonstone. But somehow it didn't look like the moonstone you saw in the picture. This stone reminded me of the pebble that I grew up seeing and playing with in Poshkhurdsoy, my village. I thought that maybe there were a lot of rocks that the astronaut picked up, and this was one of them. Or did it happen because of the palm of the people? Because the moonstone had its own warmth, some kind of strange temperature."

These are the experiences of the author, who dreamed of seeing a lifetime, and later saw that moonstone in his hand. All of us have been given to dreams and sweet dreams since childhood. Some of them we get, some we don't. As we grow older, our childhood dreams seem ridiculous. A dream leads a person to a goal. He will lead you forward.

If you achieve your dream, the above experiences may pass through your heart. Because you achieved your dream, now it seems simple to you. The most important thing is that that dream leads you to the goal. This story describes the author's hidden childhood dreams, travel impressions, and inner experiences.

In the story "Stone" the author's memory related to the stone is described. The pebble he received as a gift from Zarabog, one of the Kohitang mountain villages, or rather, from an old woman, reminds him of his childhood memories and experiences of that time: "The old woman very politely seated me around the table and surrounded me. And on the table, as usual, a stone, stone almond, this stone would appear to bite them. "

The stone was given to the author as a souvenir from this old woman. Every time he gets hold of this stone, strange memories are awakened in him. It gives the impression that the stone acts as a link between the past and the future. The pebble, which was found by the old woman many years ago from the foot of the mountain, was one of the most important everyday items of the ancient people. An archaeologist friend of the author claims that the age of this stone goes back to one hundred and fifty thousand years. As a wonder of the world, this ancient rock still serves today.

Although the story "Blue Stones" is autobiographical in nature, it reminds you of the "magical realism" of Latin American literature. After reading the story, you will be sure that this world is full of secrets and miracles. The imagination arises as if these events do not happen in real life. But you believe the author, you follow him, you are just as amazed as he is.

The story "Koktashlar" begins like this: "I go home and browse the encyclopedia. I open pages related to stone. People, rivers, streams, cities, villages, birds, trees, fruits, animals, dishes, even

flowers are associated with the name of this stone. There is even a word called Stone in Russian - kamennyy tsvetok... Is there a place without a stone? It was shown on TV, somewhere, I don't remember... When I see a field, land, square without stones, those places seem strange to my eyes. I don't know why. Maybe, I didn't know if my childhood was spent in Poshkhurdsoy, which is full of stones, or if our yard is not very rocky, but the place where the ancient koriz passed through one end - dongtepa is full of stones, I can't imagine the world without stones."
Even now, in many villages, a stone is placed on a new grave as a sign. The writer, who lost his mother at the age of 8, also places blue stones on the grave together with his brothers. The writer is also interested in why it is blue stone. "Perhaps this is related to the images of the Blue God worshiped by our ancestors," the author concludes. There is a character of Gulistan momo in the story. Momo Gulistan, who wears a brown-red dress with black stripes, fringes, and almond prints, reminds us of the old witch from fairy tales. The author, who went to the stream with his brothers to bring a bluestone to his mother's grave, fell asleep in a shelter on the way back: "When I opened my eyes, Gulistan momo was standing on top of me. "My giants said that a black snake is trying to take your breast. Look, I

killed him," he said solemnly. I looked around and got scared. A black snake was lying next to me." Take your stone, - ordered the old woman, - Remember, always take messages from this stone. He guards your mother's soul. This stone was once a heavenly angel who served the Heavenly Father.

Images, legends and stories related to giants, fairies, and snakes are widespread in folk mythology. Of course, it is hard to believe that the above reality will happen in real life. But the story of "Blue Stones" is not an artistic texture, a story with fantastic elements. This is an autobiographical, memoir-story.

This world is full of mysteries and miracles. You may encounter them at every step. But sometimes we don't follow them. Gulistan momo's foresight, ability to anticipate danger is amazing. After all, it is true that a fortune teller like Vanga lived in real life. We believe that Gulistan Momo has a divine medium that connects the real world with the unreal world. The philosophy of life and death, universe and man is put forward in the story "Blue Stones".

In general, Nadir Normatov's stories from the "My stone epics" series describe the writer's memories and experiences. It is appropriate to call these stories memory stories. All of them are bound by a stone. But the goal of the writer is not to simply describe and describe events, memories and experiences. Perhaps the example of a simple stone is to show that nature is full of mysteries, that nothing is created in vain, that our life is full of miracles and coincidences.

It is known that in the 70s and 80s of the 20th century, the story, which is a small genre of prose, seemed to be lagging a little, and many creators began to use their pen more effectively in the short story or novel genre. But literary critics and critics have recognized that the young writers who entered the literature in this genre brought a new tone, a new style, and breath. About this genre and its possibilities, U. Normatov writes: "A story has the power to express and reveal the great truth of life, the essence of a person, his character in a compact, dense form. It is not by chance that the story is compared to an aphorism, a proverb, which is considered as an expression of people's experience. One can always find a topic and material for a story, only if it is paid attention to, if real talents turn to this genre, then it will continue to show its results.

Abdugafur Rasulov comments on the storytelling of this period: "In the stories of young people, there are more and more positive types who are sincere, disinterested, and even get rid of their opponents." "Paper Flowers" by Kh. Sultanov, "Adam's Dream" by A. Azam, "Grandfather Dostmurad" by N. Qabul, "Kilko'prik" by G. Hotamov, "Thunderbolt" by M. Hazratkulov,

"Eyes of a Deer" by Z. A'lam, N. .Kilichev's "Yugan" stories are skillfully written and attract the reader's attention. In these stories, you feel that positive characters are sincere people, pillars of life."

It's no secret that in literary studies of this period, stereotyped ideas, positive and negative artistic image, and the social position of the subject and content were the leading principles in evaluating the artistic work. But the artistic works created by young writers, especially the stories, could not be analyzed and evaluated with such criteria.

Let's listen to these thoughts of A. Rasulov: "The animals and birds depicted in the stories do not fulfill the ideological task enough. Getting caught up in the ins and outs of marriage is the result of a superficial approach to life. It is natural that an artist can create mature stories and immortal works only if he takes a serious attitude to life and deeply studies the character of his contemporaries.

U. Normatov comments on this issue as follows: "We, literary critics, are obliged to preserve and support our literary achievements in the form of sprouts, as well as aiming for high peaks. There are such achievements in the creation of images of birds and animals in our storytelling today. The remarkable thing is that our story-writers express their attitude to the ecological problem that worries all of us today through the images of birds and animals, their relationship with humans, their unique way of life, destiny; most importantly, they strive to show the complexities of human life, to reveal important social, spiritual and moral problems, to promote reflection and reasoning about the reality of life and its complexities.

It should be said that the stories created by young artists who entered the literature in the 70s and 80s differed in terms of thematic scope, content, and attitude to reality. In particular, the smallest details of life, searching for artistic meaning even from everyday events, describing the relationships between people through the image of animals and birds are also important aspects of the storytelling of this period.

It is no exaggeration to say that the creators of this period turned the story into the most productive genre. It is known that A. Kadiri, A. Qahhor, G'Gulom, who laid the foundation stone of Uzbek storytelling, brought it to the level of the requirements of world realist traditions, while the artists who continued their traditions were Sh. Kholmirzaev, M.M. Dost, E. Azam, N. Normatov. , the works of H. Sultans also became a novelty in our national storytelling. In particular, "Where are you, sound of joy?", "A mare's diet", "Riverside, meadow", "Blue door", "Secret of the world", "One day there was an ant", "Birds flew from the cliff", "Yo, Jamshid Stories such as !, "Nomus" are also products of that period. According to the writer and literary critic H. Dostmuhammad, "These same works broke the tradition of troublemaking, coercion, exhortation, and not giving free rein to our literature." More importantly, the primitiveness of black and white was exposed in the example of these works. It should be noted that the work of the above writers is free from narration and exhortation, impartiality, naturalness, variety, psychological analysis in relation to reality is one of the special features of the story writing of this period.

Of course, in the prose of Uzbek literature, the story has its own classic traditions. The well-known writer Abdulla Qahhor rightfully brought this genre to the top. Later, Shukur Kholmirzaev became an active writer in the narrative genre and further expanded its possibilities. While artistically reflecting the subtlest aspects of the human heart, Adib founded a new tradition with his stories based on psychological analysis and national color.

Murad Mohammad Dost, Erkin A'zam, Khayriddin Sultan, Nodir Normatov, who brought a new tone to Uzbek literature, received the attention and recognition of literary studies and criticism in the 80s. These artists first of all tried to prove that the main task of literary studies is human studies. In this way, they searched tirelessly, diligently studied the works of classic representatives of Uzbek and world literature. After all, as Sh. Kholmirzaev pointed out: "The problem of problems is man. By truly reflecting a person in a work of art, problems arise from his actions. Solving these problems is not the writer's job. Life will decide it. And that process of resolution can find its reflection in literature."

The most important feature of the literature of the 70s and 80s that we are talking about is the deeper artistic development of the hero's soul rather than showing his place in society. As noted by the famous Russian storyteller Yuri Kazakov, "The task of literature is to express the experiences of the human heart. That is the reason why Leo Tolstoy is still the main figure in our Russian literature. Nobility, landowners, serfdom - all this is a long past, but works about them are still read with interest. Because Tolstoy reflects the human heart. Such works never get old.

Nodir Normatov, a member of the literary generation of the 70s and 80s, also actively created stories. The influence and creative experience of famous representatives of world literature such as E. Hemingway, R. Tagore, N. Gogol, L. Tolstoy, A. Chekhov, Yu. Kazakov, V. Shukshin, V. Rasputin had a significant influence on the formation of N. Normatov as a writer. In particular, it would not be wrong to say that Vasiliy Shukshin's work had a significant impact on Uzbek literature. It is known that Vasily

Shukshin started a new direction in Russian literature in "rural prose". Literary critics and critics have acknowledged that he fully revealed the true landscape of the Russian countryside, the character, psychology, nature and character of the villagers. As Yulduz Hoshimova noted: "Vasily Shukshin describes rural life truthfully and accurately in his works. This is due to the author's familiarity with the way of life of ordinary people, as well as his careful observation of language and language. The wealth of the spiritual world, universal human values are of primary importance in the lines of the writer. Most of Shukshin's heroes are ordinary workers, peasants, each of them has his own character, sour language. Some of the characters are somewhat delusional and live in their own world, while others tend to show some courage." For example, his stories included in the collection of stories "Old Man, Girl and Sun" depict village life and people.

"Village prose" also occupies an important place in N. Normatov's work. Even in the first stories of the writer, the Shukshin spirit can be observed. This is especially evident in the stories included in the creator's collection of "Kohitang stories". The main theme of the stories included in this collection is rural life, the joys and sorrows of the people of this land, dreams and aspirations. N. Normatov describes the life of the people of

Kohitang highland villages, because the writer knows these lands very well, he spent his childhood in these places.

We know that the people of the village are a bit naive, clumsy, lazy, but sincere in nature. In the village, almost everyone knows each other, human qualities such as kindness, consideration, and honor are stronger among people. National characteristics, customs and traditions, local environment are more clearly visible in the village.

In general, Nadir Normatov and Vasiliy Shukshin have one thing in common. It is known that Vasiliy Shukshin was not only a writer but also a film director and actor. He shot a number of films and wrote scripts. He himself played a number of roles. Shukshin's characters are simple, simple, ordinary people. He paints the inner experiences of his character like an artist. He feels and lives in the hearts of each of his characters. When a writer picks up a pen as a writer, it is certainly possible for him to deeply feel cinema and art, to feel the most subtle aspects of people's psyche.

Nadir Normatov also feels fine art. He organized exhibitions as a photographer, and created a number of studies as an art critic. The photographer captures situations and circumstances that the ordinary human eye could not see. The character of the human nature is shown in the images created by the artist, he paints the experiences of his hero like an artist.

If Shukur Kholmirzaev and Erkin Azam Boysun, Togay Murad Khojasaat entered our literature as a literary place, Nadir Normatov described Poshkhurd, where he was born and grew up, in his works. In almost all of his works, we come across the image of Poshkhurd and Pashkhurd people, their life, thoughts and dreams.

In the story "On the Mountain" by Nadir Normatov, the scenery of a mountain village appears before our eyes: "I entered a small village between the mountains. Low and high courtyards were seen along the stream. The water is spreading in the lower part of the valley, from which the water gradually rises and soaks into the air, and sometimes the breeze drives it towards the snow-covered glade on the side of the stream.

The villagers I'm looking for are far away. Because everything is white, it is not known that he came in late. Dogs barked in the distance. Then I noticed that the sun was setting. Because dogs return from the steppe at sunset. I had not even left the village when my boots were covered with snow. I lit a cigarette and continued walking along the winding mountain road. As my feet began to freeze, I involuntarily turned towards the last yard. There is no gate to the courtyard. I was about to go straight in, when a horseman appeared on the path at the foot of the garden. He is wearing a short coat, a t-shirt on his head, and the tip of his shoulder-mounted rifle is blackened. It looked like Cherkas described by Lermontov." Adib describes the color of the village through impressive details. The landscape of the village is clearly visible before our eyes. The author pays attention to the smallest details in describing the landscape. "Dogs barked from far away. Then I noticed that the sun was setting. Because dogs return from the steppe at sunset. If we pay attention to this passage, we can see that the writer convincingly describes the village life and environment.

Reality is told in the language of the author. Vosid sniper hosts the hero of the story in his house. Vosid hunter, whose original profession is a hunter, initially makes an impression on both the hero of the story and the reader as a "worker" of nature and animals. But during the conversation, it turns out that these thoughts are wrong: "Being a hunter myself, I rarely shot anything except a wolf and a boar."

In the following places, we will witness that Vasid sniper remained faithful to his faith. Even though the sick old woman is fond of venison, Wasid cannot shoot her during the hunting season. In general, the story describes the life of a mountain village and the hospitable, honest, faith-based people who live there.

Another characteristic of N. Normatov's stories is the artistic expression of spiritual problems. Humanity, honesty, faithfulness to one's faith, human dignity, the strength of honor, in general, various human problems and relationships that exist in real life are covered in them. These stories describe the life and character of people with various fates.

Nadir Normatov's story "Birds flew from the cliff" describes the problem of human spirituality, morals, and honor.

Rajab, the hero of the story, likes to boast lamely. But he is not proud of himself, but of his great ancestors, whose name was once passed on to his ancestors. Especially his love for his brother Beknazar. Beknazar is the director of the economy. Rajab's head reaches to the sky as another person with honor and reputation emerges from the crippled clan. The villagers know well that his brother has a big contribution to his brother's achievement. He is even ready to give his life for his brother. When he was young, he fell from a tree to pick mulberries for Beknazar and got the name lame. But his brother, who trusted him, made him famous in front of the people: "Rajab Cholak learned the following from his words: Aunt Sonia's daughter lived in the village, attended the school in the center of the farm and worked as a teacher. The economic center is three to four miles from the village of

Poshkhurd. Recently, one of the houses in the center of the economy became vacant. He found out about this and met the right commandant. "Ask the director of the farm for a mouthful, if he says yes, it's yours," said the commandant. Rachel met Beknazar. Beknazar said to him: "If I ask something, won't you say no?" "Okay," said Rachel naively. "What is he?" And Beknazar said: "Let's meet you at that house." Rachel left crying. Then he told this to his mother. When Rachel said this, Chori was also sick. He is next door to aunt Sonia. Chori went directly to the director the next day. He pulled out a snake from his bosom and signed the paper on giving Rachel a house."

The story describes the mental state of Rajab the lame, who learned about these words: "...Rajab the lame went to the grass and lay down on his back. For some reason, Rajab wanted to turn into a child and scream and cry. He knew why. He came and stood in front of Sonia, yes, Sonia, who stole her peace at that time. His brother killed him in honor! Rajab was surprised: his eyes were full of tears. He took a napkin from his pocket and wiped his tears. "Even though I'm old," he thought, "They say that when a person gets old, they cry." He was so sad that he shed many tears. Finally. The sun was shining. He got up and walked towards his grazing horse.

In the mentality of the Uzbek people, being dishonored and being a slave is one of the most severe punishments. Not being able to hold your head high in front of your friends and fellow villagers is like death for Rajab the cripple. Because he was proud of the reputation of his ancestors in front of his friends and kept his height upright. In the story, the writer does not dwell on the image of the farm director Beknazar. But we can learn how corrupt his spiritual world is from his one action. His immorality causes his brother's tragedy. Beknazar is contrasted with the lame character of his brother Rajab. The character and outlook of the brothers are different. Rajab orli, honorable, proud. And Beknazar appears before our eyes as a person who sells honor, pride, and reputation for his own selfishness.

Rajab, who was laughed at by his fellow villagers, tragically died after falling into a ravine with his lame horse. The writer shows that the cause of this tragedy is moral depravity, immorality. In the story "Birds flew from the cliff" by Nadir Normatov, the national spirit, the unique character of our people was reflected through the image of the crippled Rajab.

The writer's story "Deaf Momo" describes the spiritual image of a person, conflicts in relationships. Madiyor, the hero of the story, works at the district communications department to deliver gifts to their addressees. Stumbles while placing gifts. At this moment, one of the gifts is torn, revealing a tweed scarf. Madiyar remembers the words of Norhol, the nanny of his wife, who takes care of his son, that he will find a tweed scarf for the old woman if he needs it and if possible, his thoughts are distracted. In this process, an internal "struggle" takes place in his nature. The writer describes this process of struggle in reality. Madiyor, who went on a day's vacation with his boss, meets Kar momo to bring grapes. During a conversation with her, he learns the history of the enmity between his son's nanny Norkhol old woman and Deaf Momo, that the nanny is actually engaged in speculation and sells tweed scarves: "Who is Norkhol old woman! To whom did he entrust the upbringing of his child? To a robber, a speculator old woman. Does it get any more stupid than that? Why did he hand over his child to this old woman without asking? There are old women in the world like Kar Mama. Why doesn't he look for such people?'

For this reason, Madiyor refrains from the thought of taking the tivit scarf, that is, from the "crime" - theft. Through this story, the author points to the fact that a person's ego starts doing impure things. Madiyar Kar momo refuses to steal. Problems related to human spirituality, harmony with social and moral issues are shown in the story "Kar Momo". At first glance, Aunt Norkhol is depicted as an image of a rich woman. Deaf mom also knits woolen scarves and earns money. So, it seems that both old women are interested in wealth. It is true that in the context of the era, environment and system in which the story was created, today's commercialism was seen as a crime of speculation. Or it was not possible to do business or to collect excess state. But from today's point of view, it should be noted that both cases are viewed positively. In general, for today's readers, neither Aunt Norkhol nor Kar Momo leave a negative impression.

The story of "Deaf Momo" has its own creation history. In general, most of the literary works have a real basis and prototypes of their characters. Mamarayim Boykulov, a close confidant of the writer from the village, pedagogue and writer, tells the following about the history of the creation of the story "Kar Momo": "In January 1982, Nodir Normatov called me and told me that he was in the village, the artist Rozi Choriev, the writers: Shukur Kholmirzaev, Nurali Qabil were with him. He invited me, saying that he had come to the village and was at the state farm hotel at the same time. The director of the state farm showed honor to the guests and filled the table with goodies despite the fact that it was winter. An intense debate about art, literature, and the press began, and the conversation grew hotter and hotter. Among the talks, there were arguments about Poshkhurd delicacies, especially sweet-sugar grape varieties,

Poshkhurd technology of making molasses and musallas.

The director of the state farm praised Poshkhurd's "black Nahal" grape and said that this grape was a treasure of Bukhara emirs in ancient times. The writer Shukur Kholmirzaev said: "During my life, I have never met grapes as sweet as Boysun grapes." Together with Nadir Normatov, we went to several houses in the middle of the night and finally brought two kilos of grapes from Momo Kar Momo and put them on the table. Shukur Kholmirzaev put a few grapes in his mouth, ate them, closed his eyes and admitted: "Yes, brothers, you won." Later, Nadir Normatov used the details of this event to write a story that acquired a completely new tone and appeal. This story was published in his election "Bisot".

This reality served as an impetus and reason for expressing the artistic intention of Nadir Normatov.

In the writer's story "Whistles", the psyche of a child, his inner experiences and dreams are written. The writer shows the world of adults through the image of a child. If we look at the works of the literary generation of this period, we will come across a number of works depicting children's lives. Among them are E.Azam's stories "A man came from the city", "Farewell to a fairy tale", "Ice cream", "Watch", "Plastinka", "Memories about distant "Artek"" by Khairiddin

Sultan. Although these stories depict children's lives at first glance, they artistically express the world of adults, their concerns, and the problems of society.

"Whistles" is in harmony with the spirit of Erkin Azam's story "Farewell to the Fairy Tale". In "Farewell to the Fairy Tale" Kamil and Rachel, that is, their relationship is united by sisterhood, friendship, spiritual closeness, the same process is observed in "Whistles". When Rachel gets married, Kamil realizes that he has lost his closest confidant. This is what happens to Suyun and her step-sister Sharofat in "Whistles". Sharofat made whistles for his brother, and Suyun played them with interest. He also learned to make a whistle from his sister. But when Sharofat's sister ran away with her lover, Suyun went to the city to look for her. He whistles for it and pays his friend. But his father saw this and gave him a hug. Suyun's goal is to collect money and go to her sister. He goes out secretly, buys perfume for his sister. His sister welcomes him. Suyun gives one of the whistles she made to her sister. He thought that his sister would take the whistles and play them, and be happy. But Sharofat just puts them in the closet. "My sister doesn't love me," he suddenly thought. "When he saw well, he would whistle." He took the whistles one by one, but put them back. He wanted to take his whistles and go to the village right now, but he wanted his sister to play one day at a time. Sighing, he put on his slippers and ran out into the street. He didn't even hear his sister say, "Suyunjon, where are you?" Now the boy joined the stream of people, and it seemed to him that he could hear the clear, playful sound of a whistle from afar. Whistles. He doesn't whistle anymore, he never will."

A child's world is complicated. He believes in everything. If he finds out that he has been deceived, he will be broken. The story reveals the child's mental evolution.

Uzbek novelists are following a century-long historical path. Abdulla Qadiri founded the first Uzbek realistic novel with his novel "Otkan Kunlar", and hundreds of works have been created in this genre. Uzbek literature is enriched with colorful novels according to the scope of the topic, form, idea, content and poetic nature. After A. Qadiri's novels "Gone Days", "Mehrobdan Chayan", Cholpon's "Night and Day", A. Qahhor's "Mirage", Oybek's "Navoi", A. Mukhtar's "Plantain", O'Hoshimov's "Between Two Doors", "Starry Nights" by P. Kadirov, "Treasure of Ulugbek" by O. Yaqubov, "Lolazor" by M.M. Dost, "Fields left by my father" by T. Murad, "A Thousand Faces" by O. Mukhtar, "Noise" by E. Azam, Novels such as "Bazaar" by H. Dostmuhammad and "Muvozanat" by U. Hamdam showed the wide possibilities of this genre. Most of the above novels were created during the Mustabid Shura era. But they differ sharply from other works created on the basis of the ideology of the Shura period.

In the late 80s and early 90s of the last century, a new era of Uzbek novels began. According to D. Kuronov, "Since the 90s of the last century, there has been a sharp increase in the weight of artistic conventionality in the poetic arsenal of our national prose, an increase in works built on the basis of symbolic and figurative images, and a wide range of modernist research." In fact, by the 70s and 80s, in our national literature, in particular, in our prose, there was a search for the creation of new forms and methods of artistic expression. D. Kuronov cites the following reason as one of the main factors that caused this: "If from the second half of the 70s, the desire to tell the truth about the state of society has become the main trend in our literature, then in the conditions of transparency, the press has fully taken over this mission and has begun to achieve it more and more." Now, no matter how truthfully it reflects life, it has become certain that literature cannot compete with journalism in terms of relevance, truthfulness, and analysis. In the same situation, creative research aimed at finding new forms and methods of artistic expression, which can reveal its identity to literature, find its place and restore its position, has intensified. Belonging to the literary generation of the 70s and 80s, Nodir Normatov started new poetic research in the early period of his work. In particular, in the story "Once upon a time there was an ant..." he created an example of a fictional work in Uzbek literature using the tool of artistic conditionality. In the short story "Bisot" he skillfully used psychologism to express the inner feelings of a person, while in "The Man Under the Tree" he expressed his artistic intention through the means of mythological views, condition-trial in Uzbek folklore, and artistic conditionality.

Nadir Normatov grew in creative pursuits. He created his first novel "Barigal" in the early 90s. The writer himself expresses these thoughts about this work: "My next book, the novel Barigal, was published in 1991 by Kamalak publishing house. Until then, the book manuscript was discussed at the Writers' Union under the leadership of Said Ahmed. The work was approved and recommended to the "Eastern Star" magazine. Said Ahmed objected to the name of the novel: The name is too light, if you find another name. The teacher was ill and could not read the manuscript. I did not change the name of the work. "Barigal" is a Khorezm song, it has its own history. Barigal means come back. I have long been interested in the image of a person appealing to his heart. It is a great salve for some of today's selfish people. The scope of the work is wide: events take place in Surkhandarya, Tashkent, St. Petersburg. During the discussion, Usman Azim, Erkin Azam, Asad Dilmurod spoke in full approval of the novel, only advised to shorten it a little. In this regard, Ibrahim Gafurov writes: "The novel "Barigal" by the writer, art critic, expert of folk art Nodir Normatov was published in 1989-1990, when the reconstructions of the last century were in full swing and the efforts of national states to gain independence peaked and entered a decisive period. It was published in the year 2008 and reached the hands of readers... ... Twenty years after the first edition of the work, Nadir came up with the idea of republishing it and presenting it to the current readers under the name "Two in the Mirror" and began to prepare for it. By preparation, we mean that the author added new chapters to this work, filled the life of the characters, enriched it with new lines. He carefully edited the parts that seemed boring to him." We based our research on the republished version of "Twins in the Mirror". The novel "Twins in the Mirror" has its own characteristics in its artistic essence and compositional structure. The novel consists of three parts and each of them has separate chapters. In each chapter, a specific reality, the fate of the hero is told, and they together form the general plot line of the novel. In the novel, the

lives, thoughts, dreams, dreams, and pain of several characters
"Maybe you can take me home"
"I can't do that, Princess.
You yourself left home.
Now come back yourself.
Then it will be right."
"Maybe you don't love me...
That's why..." "No, Princess. My heart is with you.
 But come home yourself.
I will not go and fetch you.'
 "I was coming back home. But something is holding me back."
"What is it?" "I don't know either.
Maybe it's the devil.
That's why it would be good if you told me: come down to me, go home.
" "How can I say? People say that he begged his wife and brought him home.
How I'm holding my head up in the pan.
It's better for you to enter the yard by yourself, in front of people, as if to say, "Here I left, I'm back."
"I'll do it like that, I don't have enough strength."
"What can I do to get stronger?"
"That... thing... Give up Dangona..."
"You know I can't do that... It's my father's will."
 My grandfather has an isnad. In order to wash it, I have to fulfill the will."

"What about me? Don't you think of me? Ask me how much I have to say?
"Say, what are you talking about?"
"No... I can't say... I can't..."
"The day will come when you will be able to speak your mind, Princess." "I don't know.
I don't know what I'm doing."

Although they try to reconcile with each other, they lack determination and courage in this way. The character of Karajan is included in the novel. It appears in some parts of the work. The princess accidentally sees Karajan in the bathroom, falls in love with him and wants to be with him. At the end of the play, he manages to be with Karajan himself and betrays Omar. In fact, when Malika saw Karajan for the first time, there were cracks and fissures in her heart. In the novel "The Two in the Mirror", the mirror played the role of an important detail. At the beginning of the work, the legend of the mirror is given from the language of Omar's mother. If we observe N. Normatov's work, we can see that he effectively uses folklorism to express his artistic intention. This brings to mind the style of artistic expression in Chingiz Aitmatov's work. In particular, in the short story "Aq kema" and the novel "The Day of the Century" literary legends are widely used.

The legend that Nadir Normatov introduced into the novel ensured the full artistic output of the work. This legend concerns the fate of the heroes of the work. At this point, we considered it appropriate to quote the legend from the work: "Once upon a time there was a young man. He lived in our Pana. This young man went to India to learn glassmaking. An apprentice fell to a master without a mirror. When she had a daughter, she fell in love with that guy.

Years have passed. The master did not teach the young man the secret of glassmaking, he was deceiving him, and he did not give him his daughter. One day, that girl told the young man the secret of the master, then she begged him to like her, to make a mirror from the ashes of her body. At first, the young man did not think the girl's words were true. When the girl saw that he really burned her, she cried hard, took his ashes and added them to the clay to make a magic potion made a mirror. He dedicated the song "Barigal" to this mirror and the reflection of the girl in it. The leitmotif of the novel "Two in the Mirror" is the folk song "Barigal". The original title of the work was "Barigal". This melody echoes throughout the novel. Umar's father, Zaman Baba, also listens to this song all the time. If we look at the text of this song, we can see that it refers to the beloved land: Sansan is my darling, come on Take my life, come on! Don't give up my pain, come on! Come on, come on, come on, come on, Take my life, come on! This song gives romantic pathos to the piece. A lover suffering from longing calls his lover to him. In the novel, he performed a certain task as a dangona. First of all, this is a folk song. People's pain and dreams are embodied in it. In our opinion, this song, like Dangona, calls people who are affected by the tragedies of Shura politics to be close and united. It expresses people's way of life, solidarity, traditions and values, dreams. The mirror plays an important role in the work. The reality in the myth of the mirror is transferred to the real world. Malika, who betrayed Omar, sets herself on fire to get rid of this disgrace. Just like the girl in the legend. In the work, the mirror performs a certain task, a mission.

According to I. Yakubov, "mirror detail has a multifunctional nature in the text of this novel. Already, this detail summarizes all actions, portraits, landscapes, domestic life, life situations, mental experiences, directs the reader's attention and convinces him. So, behind this detail there is a certain reality: the domestic life of the involuntary, simple people of the village of Pana near the Mustabid center life, actions and aspirations, external and internal portrait lines, psyche, dreams are embodied. Therefore, the fate of the two in front of the mirror (Umar and Malika) is summed up by an important detail called the mirror of artistic reality. The writer's views are expressed clearly and concretely and acquire a strong expressive essence.

The author does not mention the myth of the mirror at the beginning of the novel. It was a reference to the fate of the heroes of the work, a symbol of the tragic end of the work. Because, as Chekhov said, "The gun hanging on the wall in the first act of the play must be fired at the end of the performance."

Our people have many customs and traditions related to mirrors. In particular, the custom of keeping a mirror for the bride and groom is still preserved. The mirror is called the mirror of the soul. It is impossible to know what kind of experiences and feelings are going on in a person's heart. Man appears in thousands of forms. Nadir Normatov holds a mirror to the hearts of the heroes of the novel "Two in the Mirror" and looks into their inner world.

In the novel, we meet several characters, their nature and fate. The old man is one of the complex characters. Umar confronts old man Ortiq in Kyzilgul. Umar, who first meets a lonely old man in a deserted village, likens him to Khizr. Then, during the conversation, his true self is revealed.

The old man belongs to the category of people who can save their lives and find benefits, even if it is in any vile and disgusting way. He made a living by slandering and stabbing others in the society of Soviet politics. Omar's father was also imprisoned by old man Ortiq. He mentions his work with pride. But he does not regret what he has done, even though he is old. It is true that he first meets the children and relatives of the people he hurt and apologizes to them. But he remains a believer in the ideology of false faith.

Quoted from his speech: "I am the cause of the destruction of these lands. But I don't regret it. I am one of the first people in the region to move people to the steppe" , "I lived happily among these mountains. If necessary, I have passed ninety percent of the wives of a village, nephew. I have no dreams left" , "If you don't become a man and live like a rooster, this world is forbidden for a person. "I lived in Stalin's time" shows the true image of the old man. The old man eventually dies a tragic death. Man comes to this world and wants to leave behind good deeds and good deeds. He is always given the opportunity to choose.

Someone follows the path of goodness and deserves the honorable name of human, while someone else chooses the path of evil. The old man also chose the path of evil. In fact, this part of it is caused by the authoritarian system society. Such people, brought up on the basis of false beliefs and false ideas, lived mutely and submissively. And the old man chose the easy way in life. He saw life as just fun. In this way, he did not return even disgusting deeds. Through this image, the writer personified the fate of people who are poor and have lost their human form.

Another character in the novel is Muhammad Tahir. Muhammad Tahir, a writer by profession, is originally from the village of Karakoz near Pana. Notably, Muhammad Tahir is the writer himself. The writer introduces his prototype into the work. In this, hints are given in the reality of the work. In particular, Omar writes a letter to him about his work. Umar Muhammad Tahir, the hero of Nadir Normatov's story "Bisot", is portrayed in it. The letter focuses on some errors in the story, places where the logic is broken.

The reality of the novel takes place not only in the village of Pana, but also in Leningrad and Tashkent. When Umar goes to Leningrad to study for a month, the scope of the topic also expands. A bit off topic from Pana. The second part of the novel begins with the events of Leningrad.

Omar makes new acquaintances here. On the plane, he meets Azim Seistani, an orientalist from Afghanistan. Mohammad Tahir meets Umar in Leningrad. Muhammad Tahir's goal is to see the magic mirror kept in the Hermitage. Because he came here to create a fictional story based on a historical event involving a mirror. Omar sees that mirror in the Hermitage. He likens this mirror to the one his mother gave to Malika. When Umar told Muhammad Tahir about this, he wanted to go and see the mirror. Muhammad Tahir's fictional story "Babur's Mirror" is included in the novel. Adib used the composite molding method here. This story is related to the legend of the mirror, which Muhammad Tahir brings to life in his imagination. The story of "Babur's Mirror" is based on a legend told by Omar's mother. The author of the story connects the magic mirror with the Babur family.

The next scenes of the novel are presented through the eyes of Muhammad Tahir. The events of Leningrad are directly transferred to Tashkent. They describe the daily life, family, thoughts, and inner experiences of Muhammad Tahir.

One of the bright characters in the novel is Halima, a gambler. He has his own past, bitter fate. At first, Halima the gambler gives us the impression of a negative character. The author Halima does not disclose the real image and character of the gambler. Just like detective works, the puzzles of Halima the Gambler are not solved quickly. Usually, it has been a stereotype to divide the characters into positive or negative characters in the work of art. When we say a gambler, we imagine a criminal. We label such individuals as negative heroes. What about actually? We do not listen to his inner world. We do not speculate about the reasons for the crime.

As we learn about Halima the gambler's bitter fate and past experiences, our attitude towards her changes. Halima, whose real name is Karasoch, who spent her youth years in the construction of the Ferghana Canal, lived in wandering, lived patiently when her husband was imprisoned, entered the path of gambling against her will. The old man will change his fate. It ruins his sweet marriage. Her husband imprisons Avazmand. Halima gambles with the gambler's father-in-law, Ortiq Sarik, and loses two bracelets left by her mother. Ordiq bequeaths to Karasoch that his son Avazmand will win these bracelets when his son Avazmand comes to Karasoch. But Avazmand also returns from prison sick. It cannot execute a will. Karasoch performs this task. Before his death, Avazmand left the following will to his wife Karasoch: "Karasoch," he said, "you are a lucky player, you will rob all the thieves and big boys." Teach my sons to gamble too. Until there is equality in this country, you too live a hard life. I lived honestly and got like this. Come on, I'd know if I got better. If I tell you what I saw and knew in prison, your heart will burst and die."

In the above cries that burst out from the chest of Awazmand, the true nature of the society of the authoritarian system is revealed. Halima's path as a gambler is not right. But this path was his bitter fate, revenge for the injustices of the society, for what he had experienced, from the society, from those who caused it. At the end of the play, he and Muhammad Tahir return to the place where he was born and raised, that is, to his own self. Most importantly, he does not lose his humanity. In the novel, we will encounter many more characters. Omar's brother Ismat dies tragically because of his selfishness and careerism.

Omar's friend Sultan makes a warm impression with his sincere, simple, open and humble. Especially his relationship with his wife Marjona is enviable. The villagers named these two couples Laili and Majnun. The Sultan is embodied as an image that always shares goodness with people.

In general, Nadir Normatov demonstrated a wide range of realism in the novel "Two in the Mirror". In it, he showed man not only as a product of social relations, but as a divine unity of being.

There are many works created on the basis of biographical method in world literature. French artists such as St. Beauvais and Andrey Morois created the first works in this genre and gained fame. Saint Beauvais is one of the scientific and theoretical founders of the biographical method in literary studies. This method, as noted by the literary critic Bahadir Karim, "should not be understood simply as a biography. Indeed, the biographical method is not a simple chronological description and classification of the creator's biography; the year of birth of the writer, the place or environment where he lived, the year of writing of his works and, finally, the year of the death of the creator - all these are considered biographical information.

What is the biographical method? To find an answer to this question, we turn to the opinion of B.Karim: "The biographical method is based on a pair of writers and works of art. He pays serious attention to the creator's personal life, living environment, mental and psychological state, personal interests, inspiration factors that motivated him to write the work, the creator's laboratory and a number of historical and individual issues.

A biographical work can be short story, novel, historical or other forms. Autobiographical works also rely on the same method. For example, "Tales from the past" by A. Qahhor, "Childhood" by Oybek, etc.

In a biographical work, documentary, truthfulness and impartiality are the leaders. At its center is a person and his life. Usually, the hero of a biographical work is a famous person. If the hero of the work is familiar, contemporary, there is no difficulty for the author. For the author, every detail about his character is important. For example, the letter, memory, diary, belongings, etc. of the hero of the work.

The author of the biographical work, first of all, is required to be careful, not to falsify information, and to be impartial. Although Irving Stone's thoughts about biographical narratives apply to all biographical works: "The author of a biographical narrative should be a biographer who works to collect material about a person or a group of people. It is necessary for him to master the complex technique of classifying these materials, to find a special style manual suitable for each situation, a special style of writing in order to distinguish this one from the hundreds of millions of different life events that have happened to people."

Artistic expression of the hero's experiences in the novel "Rozy Choriev's last will"

Among the works created on the basis of the biographical method in Uzbek literature, the biographical novel "Rozi Choriev's Last Testament" by Nadir Normatov stands out. N. Normatov is not only a writer, but also an art critic who has written many articles on fine and applied art, conducted research. In addition, the author had many conversations with the hero of the work, Rozi Choriev, and accompanied her on trips. It is known from N. Normatov's memoirs written at the end of the book that he was with the artist even in the last days of his life and fulfilled his wills. Rozi Choriev entrusts the implementation of his will to N. Normatov, he trusts him. Because, on the one hand, the writer became like his native neighbor, on the other hand, both artists were born in the village of Pashkhurd, Sherabad district of Surkhandarya. There is no doubt that this also brought them closer together.

The book reveals the life and creative activity of Rozi Choriev. N. Normatov explains the reason for the creation of this work as follows: "... One day, brother Rozi said:
- At many meetings, especially children tell me how you became an artist. I tell them that I became an artist by studying. I would say that drawing incessantly made me an artist at this

level... But I feel that these words are not enough. If they write a book together and this book is the answer to their questions...

This was the motivation, and I started writing the artist's thoughts on art and life. At first I wanted to write on behalf of Rozi brother. Then, when I looked, what I knew about the artist, what I heard and observed began to flow into him. As a result, the work was formed from the point of view of the artist and the author. Term: a third point of view - the student has a new view and opinion about art and life, that's the important thing.

People's writer of Uzbekistan Erkin Azam writes about the creation of this work: "It was the duty of Nadir Normatov to write this book. Rozi Choriev was a person worthy of being the hero of such a wonderful work. Nadir knew this artist closely. This work is a symbol of my writer friend's true respect for the great artist.

About the creation of this work of Nodir Normatov, his villager, close confidant, pedagogue Mamarayim Boykulov writes: "Since 1963, Nadir Normatov has been engaged in studying, researching and promoting the life and work of the People's Artist of Uzbekistan Rozi Choriev in the mass media.

He wrote several articles about the artist, the documentary story "The House Where the Rainbow Lived", and later the novel-essay "The

Last Testament of Rozi Choriev". These works, which illuminate the life and creative activity of the great artist from his childhood to the end of his life, did not appear by themselves. After work, Nadir Normatov goes to the artist's studio almost every day, he witnesses conversations and creative dialogues that last until midnight. was".

Berdi Rahmat also commented on this work: "... in 2008, the writer published another new novel of his. It is called "Rozi Choriev's last will". This work is also about the life and work of the great artist. There are many novels and stories about the life and work of great artists in world literature. These works leave a great impression on the reader about the life of those painters, the process of creating the paintings by their brushes, their unique history, and their place in world painting.

There was no such perfect work about artists in Uzbek literature until now. This novel by Nadir Normatov filled this gap. As soon as this work was published, it gained the attention of creative people in a short time.

The biographical novel "The last will and testament of Rozi Choriev" was recognized by the general public, literary critics, artists and writers, and art historians. Soon the book was translated into Russian by N. Normatov's wife Gavhar Normatova. The Russian translation was published in "Zvezda Vostoka" magazine in 2011 and 2012. In 2015, it was published as a book by "Uzbekistan" publishing house.

Art critic Akbar Hakimov says the following about this book: "It was necessary to write this book. The portrait of R. Choriev depicted in the work reflects and further enriches our culture. This is a unique book written with high poetic skills. In addition, the novel-essay is an artistic work with an extremely interesting narrative style.

If we look at the history of Uzbek literature, a number of works were created in the "Life of wonderful people" series. Among them, we can include novels-essays such as "Abdulla Qahhor" by O. Sharafiddinov, "Cholpon" by N. Karimov, and "Maqsud Shaikhzoda".

It can be said that Nadir Normatov's novel-essay "Rozi Choriev's Last Testament" was a novelty in Uzbek literature with its unique composition, style of expression, and form. The author does not follow the path of a dry description of the artist's biography. Reflecting the artist's life from childhood to his death, Adib uses memories, conversations with him and notes in his notebook. The events in the play complement each other. Sometimes the artist's memories, conversations or thoughts are given, sometimes the writer's observations, what he knows, what he witnessed. But they don't get mixed up or confused. The history of creation of the artist's works will not leave the reader indifferent. These are told through the artist's memories and conversations. Importantly, "Rozi Choriev's last will" does not bore the reader. A complete portrait of Rozi Choriev is presented in the novel-essay. The novel consists of three parts. The first part is called "The house where the rainbow lives." It describes the artist's childhood, his teachers, his memories of his first introduction to art, and his childhood difficulties. In the part called "The last days of the artist" Rozi Choriev's views on life and art, thoughts, travel impressions are reflected. The third part of the book "Rozi Choriev's last will" contains the events after the artist's death, the memories and notes of his contemporaries.

Interesting in its composition, this biographical novel-essay takes the reader into the strange world of art. In it, the great artist Rozi Choriev's personality, delicate taste, character, inner world, history of creation of his works will be told. For this, the writer effectively uses various tools and details.

The important factors that determine the success of this biographical novel are as follows:

First, the author, first of all, the writer. So far, he has gained fame as the author of a number of fiction works - stories, short stories, and novels. Adib is well aware of the laws of art and has his own style. A writer's writing skills come in handy when creating a novel-essay. Because he describes even ordinary realities as a work of art, embodies the character of Rozi Choriev, his inner experiences, feelings, and character to the smallest detail.

Secondly, the author has a delicate sense of art. His many articles and researches about art, history of art, life of great artists prove our opinion. These works of Rozi Choriev help to reveal its essence, to illuminate the image of the artist as an artist.

Thirdly, Nadir Normatov had many conversations with the hero, was a companion, and knows the history of the creation of a number of the artist's works.

Each part of the novel consists of separate chapters and they are named. The first part of the novel "The last will and testament of Rozi Choriev" "The house where the rainbow lives" is written mainly in the form of dialogue. The interlocutors are the artist and the author of the novel. "The door of the color of impressions" given as an introduction to the work begins with a landscape: "The village of Vandob is located at the foot of the mountain. Summer comes here quite late. Rather, he is in no hurry to collect the spring dowry. After all, such a scene is formed: spring is fading away and summer is beginning.

There were days when apricots ripened in the village and the branches of the same tree turned yellow. But just like that, near the yard where we live - on the slopes of the mountain, flowers are still blooming, white, red, yellow butterflies are flying in the knee-high meadow, and if you go to the waterfall, the colors will close your eyes. You remember your childhood. What a pleasure it is to enter the dense thicket and dream! You will gasp at the scent of fragrant flowers. You can hear the chirping of birds.

I was sitting alone in the room and looking at these scenic pictures that I had painted yesterday.

Brother Rozi has been working since morning on the edge of the yard, on the roof of the straw-walled house, the boy eating apricots, the view of the distant hills.

When the author describes the creative process of the artist and the landscape of nature, the reader hints that a great artist is standing before his eyes. The artist is busy creating a work. He is inspired by nature and the environment. Rozi Choriev's works often feature nature pictures. The author expresses the first ideas about the creative process of the artist in the first line.

The artist kept a special notebook and recorded his memories, experiences, impressions, art and opinions on various topics. N. Normatov also gives notes related to the topic from this notebook. We know that Rozi Choriev's childhood was difficult. In the chapter titled "Childhood Memories", these lines from the artist's notebook about his childhood are quoted: "I don't remember my mother. He died of sweating when I was an eight-month-old baby. Soon, my father too... My aunt, who died at the age of ninety, told me this. In the years I was born, times were turbulent.

There was a famine. "Many things happened during the years when the collective farm was established. "Many, middle-class artisans, literate people who knew Arabic, and rich merchants were imprisoned without being questioned, because of people's backbiting," my aunt said. "The children of such people were left on the street, and how many died of hunger."

There was a time when people were suspicious of each other. As a result of such mistakes and injustices, many families, people, relatives, brothers, sisters, and brothers were scattered in all directions. As my aunt told me, I have experienced such trades with the old man..."

The author further fills these memories. Based on conversations with the artist, notes in the side notebook, what he heard from people who knew about the artist's parents, his childhood, he vividly revives the childhood years of R. Choriev. Adib describes it as a work of art. Young Rozi, her difficult childhood years, first dreams, first moments of creativity are embodied in front of your eyes. This style does not bore the reader. On the contrary, mere memories, figures, statements do not allow the reader to fully imagine the scenery before his eyes. It is known that Rozi Choriev's childhood was spent in an orphanage. He participates in the circle of young local historians in the orphanage. He learns the secrets of painting from a young artist named Elena.

Elena's stories about the lives of famous artists in the world, the Hermitage Museum, motivate the future artist to realize his future dreams. In the seasons "Striving for a Dream" and "Conversation near the Hermitage", Rozi Choriev's education, years of military service, and formation as an artist are told.n the "Return to the Village" season, the artist, who has been away from his native village for 33 years, comes to the village and has a number of memories about his current situation, which allows to express this reality from different angles. The memories of the author who witnessed this event are given: "After thirty-three years, the artist came to his native village Poshkhurd. I witnessed this incident. I was studying in the sixth grade at that time. Summer time. For some reason, I came to Sherabad, the district center thirty kilometers from the village. When I finished work, I was going to go home, and I was waiting at the station for a passenger horse or car to arrive. At that time, there were no buses to the village, and the mountain road was broken, narrow, and comprised of ravines, and trucks could hardly drive there. On that day, we returned to the village on the tractor of a fellow villager named Juma Hafiz. In the trailer connected to the tractor, there was me, a guy wearing a turban, and a golden-haired Russian girl next to him."

Of course, the author did not know the artist, who was still young at that time, and who left the village many years ago. Later, he learns that the person who was a passenger in the same boat with him is Rozi Choriev. Rozi Choriev himself tells about this trip: "... Thirty-three years later, I went to my native village - Poshkhurd. We drew a lot of things in the album on the way and walked ten miles to the village. But we were not well received in the village. We had a distant relative. "What are you doing marrying a Russian? He loves you now. And he will not look after you when you are old. I have seen many such people in the army," he said. I was upset with him and went to the neighboring village - Zarabok. Tears were flowing from my eyes. Even if you come to your village once in thirty-three years, it will hurt if they don't treat you well."

These lines describe Rozi Choriev's visit to his father's house: "His fellow villagers told brother Rozi that his father was a master craftsman and a skilled builder. The artist was shown the straw wall that his father had restored with his own hands...

... My father Normat Alimardonov told this story like this:

"We were sitting at home. Rozi sang: "Yaril tash, yaril tash, I'll see my mother, I'll be satisfied with my mother." Then he said to me: "I want to see my house, my yard, find them." We started it. But as he got closer to his house, he couldn't walk, his path was difficult. I understood his situation, I stayed behind so that he would be alone. But he was walking in such a way that he was not at all like the active and agile Rozi. I took his arm, we went to that yard together. The host welcomed us well. He was a guest. Rozi saw a one-room house that looked like a straw house and couldn't leave it. He knew that he was born in this house, he did not even look back at the food. He sat down and began to draw from one end. After finishing his work, the owner of the house told him: "There are vines left by your father. Now I will pick grapes from that vine for you", Rozi's eyes were filled with tears. He got up and went to the garden, stroking the vines with his hands."

Through the above three memories, a full picture of the incident of Rozi Choriev's arrival in the village is awakened. In particular, the image of the artist's inner experiences and feelings cannot be simply read. The artist's feelings such as orphanhood, hunger, wandering, travel, longing for the place where he was born and grew up, and remembering his parents are expressed.

The song "Yoril tosh-e, yoril tosh, I will see my mother, I will be satisfied with my mother" that he sang, seems to have burst out of his heart's tears, pain and suffering. Nadir Normatov absorbed the story of Rozi Choriev's return to the village in his artistic works. For example, in the short story "Jaza" there is a scene where a chief accountant and a stranger came to Mayram Koshmija's yard and they were met by Mergan Momo: "One of the guests is the chief accountant of the farm. The old woman did not recognize the person on her floor. He does not look like a man of this land from his appearance and clothes. He is young and has a beard. My hair looks like a dreamy little girl's. Momo Mergan greeted them. And the bearded man opened his arms towards the old woman, saying, "Come on, let's see each other." Momo Sniper got scared and backed away. He thought that the guest must be drunk. The chief accountant cheerfully introduced the guest. "Oh, aunt, don't be afraid, this person is the son of Chori Pakhsakash," he said.

From the above, it is not difficult to recognize the figures of Normat Alimardonov, the father of chief economic accountant Nodir Normatov, and Rozi Choriev, the son of Chori pakhsakash. Of course, in this story, reality is somewhat fictionalized. This shows that the writer effectively uses the real reality, the memories he has seen and known in the artistic work. In general, most of the heroes of Nadir Normatov's works have a real basis for their prototypes and events. It is appropriate to study the author's work from the point of view of the biographical method. Any work of art is a product of talent. The creative process is a mysterious and complex process. This process is different for each artist. It is related to the creative laboratory. Many artists point out that a true work of art is not always born. It also depends on inspiration, creative influence and other factors. The creative processes of famous artists, the history of the birth of their works, etc., have always been interesting for experts in the field. For a biographer, important material is the character, character, work style, creative process, relationship with people, conversation and correspondence.

In the "Birth of the Work", "Etude", "Picture", "The Second Life of Man", "Landscape" sections of "Rozy Choriev's last will" we are talking about the history of creation of some of Rozy Choryev's works, his comments on visual art and its genres. done The author provides this information through the notes in the artist's notebook, through conversations with him. For example, the artist's comments about the landscape are very important for young artists:

"I think that the happiest person is an artist who can sing about his country, his nature, his soil with the language of visual art. You may remember that Leonardo da Vinci was able to use the natural scenery typical of all Italy as a background in his work "Giocondo". This tradition was continued in the works of Titian, Botticelli, and De la Francesca. I am not saying this for nothing. In the works of some of our current artists, foreign color remains the main thing...

The landscape is valuable for me primarily as a genre that gives life to a person and reflects the image of our Mother Earth - our planet. It is clear to everyone that a person needs not only the beauty of the landscape, but above all the Mother-Earth, who provides him with a gentle blessing...

... The landscape has tones, color, harmony, documentation. If you pay attention to the works of Shishkin, a Russian artist, a master of the landscape genre, you can notice more documentary. But the artist gave this documentary a sense of feeling nature in an upbeat spirit. As long as the artist's attitude to the landscape and nature is not reflected, it will remain a mere image without feeling."

In the chapter called "Notes in the Author's Diary" in the novel, the author's diary notes related to the personality and creativity of Rozi Choriev for different years are included. These records began on June 12, 1968 and ended on December 1986. The first note gives the author's first impression of the artist: "I came to Rozi Choriev's workshop. He received me in a nervous state. He seems like a very bad person. Can I not come? But I liked the pictures of his workshop. Especially the portrait of "Batir Zakirov". The singer is in a crimson fire, as if such colors are burning in his bosom. The singer looks tired, nervous..."

Of course, this is the first impression of the author, who is still a student, in the artist's workshop. Later, it is known that N. Normatov often visited this workshop and became the closest confidant of the artist. These two artists are united not only by being born in the same village, but also by creativity. Adib wrote down the meeting with the artist, the conversations he had during the trips, and the impressions he got from his works. Here's another note. This note is dated December, 1985: "Rangtasvir always plays the role of a 'bridge' in connecting the human heart with existence." This "bridge" is elegant, solid and legal...

I came to this idea after watching Rozi Choriev's "Music of Surkhandarya" today.

- Writer Shukur Kholmirzaev also liked this work. "This work is in the museum," says the artist.

The second part of the work is called "The Last Days of the Artist". In this section, the author, researcher Feruza Khajiyeva, noted: "Entering the mind of his character Rozi Choriev, he fills in some empty points in the first part from his point of view, explains the events and connects the memories of the artist on his deathbed through an interesting chain (a bag with documents and letters serves as a chain)".

In this part, Nadir Normatov describes the life path of bedridden Rozi Choriev, his brightest memories, happy and difficult moments through the prism of his imagination.

The situation of Rozi Choriev, who is spending the last months of his life, is revealed through internal psychologism in the "Lonely" season of "The Last Days of the Artist": "Early January 2004. The weather is cold. Although the living room was well heated, the artist was lying on the sofa with his legs wrapped around the bed. His body was freezing, his brain and consciousness, on the contrary, were working like clockwork. "Why did it happen? Once when I was ready to die, God did not take my life. Now seems to be the time. "But why didn't he take my life then?", the artist thought.

It is important for an artist to create in nature, to meet people of different ages and temperaments. Travels encourage the artist to new creative experiences. Most of Rozi Choriev's life was spent on trips. It's not just a trip, it's a vacation. His brush always accompanied him wherever he went. He was engaged in painting even during his military service. Here too, he gained reputation due to his talent. In the novel-essay, the artist's memories, events, and creative processes are reflected in various corners of our country, places of residence, foreign trips. Sometimes during these trips he faced difficult and difficult situations. In the seasons of the novel-essay "Khojakent khanshda", "Strange drugs", "Feldsher" it is told that Rozi Choriev got a leg injury while going to the mountain to paint and found a cure in the house of an old man and an old woman in a nearby village. Humanity, hospitality, openness of the Uzbek people are shown in these stories.

When he injured his leg in the mountains, he sent a letter to his wife Marina: "Dear Marina! I just picked up a pen and began to write, and I confess that I forgot to write a letter... I slipped and fell on the way. I broke my shin. Now I am being treated at a doctor's house in a small village on the road leading to the village of Humson. I wrote down some of his recipes. Most importantly, I did quite a few drafts here. I am collecting details for my future paintings.

Don't worry, I'm fine now.

Greetings Rozi".

Through the letter, the writer conveys to the reader the difficulties of the artist in the way of art and creativity.

The novel also contains memoirs related to the personal family life of the artist. The "Marina" season tells the story of the artist's meeting and marriage with her husband. Fine art was the reason why he met his wife Marina: "He remembers the first time he met Marina. At that time, as usual, he studied at the institute, ran to the Hermitage in his spare time, spent hours looking at the works of Van Gogh and Rembrandt. One day, a short-haired, sheep-eyed, fair-faced girl passed by with an older woman (probably her mother). In those days, he found out that his beloved daughter had died in Tashkent through a letter sent by Sasha Botsman, and the world seemed dark to him. His friend Ahmad (he was studying sculpture) cheered him up and convinced him that painting would be better than being unfaithful.

"If this girl walks next to Rembrandt's painting "The Girl with the Falling Sunlight", I will definitely marry her," he thought. And Marina, as if she knew what he was thinking, went to this work and began to watch it." In the next pages of the book, memories and pictures related to Marina can be found.

Seasons in the section "The last days of Rozi Choriev" are shown sometimes through the eyes of the author, sometimes through the eyes of the artist. The author vividly relives the artist's memories. Realities are told not only with a simple, dry statement, facts, but also in a lively, figurative way. This is an important factor in conveying the facts to the reader in a convincing and impressive way.

As mentioned above, Rozi Choriev went on creative trips to many countries of the world. At the time, the artist also published his travel impressions in the press pages. His article "Familiar and Unfamiliar Italy" published in the pages of "Sant" magazine is devoted to the impressions of the artist's trip to Italy. This article is also attached to the book, which describes the artist's trip to the country of painters in a unique way: "...I drew about twenty pictures, drafts, sketches on the streets of Rome. The sun came up and I went to the hotel without stopping behind the mountains. The statue of Julius Caesar by the Forum followed me silently. Tomorrow I have to go to Amantea, the pride of the Italian people.

Also, in the "Vietnam" and "Sweden" chapters of the book, the artist's creative travels in these countries are told. Rozi Choriev created a number of works as a result of his creative trips to these countries.

For the biographer, the correspondence of the hero is considered one of the most important sources. Correspondence of Rozi Choriev with the artist Abdulhak Abdullaev is included in the book. These correspondences were written when Rozi Choriev was studying at the institute in Leningrad (now St. Petersburg). In addition to everyday topics, the two artists expressed interest in each other, asking how they are doing, opinions about life, art, and lessons from a teacher to a student.

Here is an example of this letter written by Rozi Choriev to Abdulhak Abdullaev:
"Hello dear brother Abdulhaq!
I was very touched to read your letter. He gave me a lot of spiritual strength. But it was very difficult to write a reply to your letter. It's not because it's difficult to answer your questions, but because I've been very busy. At that time, I started writing my thesis. I started writing the picture with inspiration. I felt really happy at that moment. I discovered many things for myself while working on my thesis. I felt that I still have a lot of searching and learning to do in the way of creativity.
Sorry, I can't argue with you. I really want to work now. I think you will understand and forgive me."
Sincerely, Rozi.
March 13, 1965"

Below is a passage from Abdulhaq Abdullaev's letter, which serves to give a general idea:

"Dear Rozi!
I received your letter. Thank you for that. I was being treated in the hospital. That's why I'm writing a late reply to your letter. I was treated for a month. I returned on February 20. You also wrote about being sick. Sorry. Everything that happens in life affects me. I know from my own

experience that in marriage, things often happen completely opposite to our wishes.
Life is a puzzle for me. We always have to look for its puzzles (of course, to the extent that we can). It is an understatement to say that "life is a science that always gives us headaches." It's more complicated than that. Smart people can't get far with creativity alone. More specifically, they say that if you are unable to observe life, your creativity will not be very deep. I don't know if you have read Repin's letters or not? There are words written in them that can be an example for us. When Repin was young, realizing that he did not study much, did not know many things, and that his knowledge was not enough, he asked Kramskoi "What should I do?" he asked for advice. According to Repin, then Kramskoy listened to him attentively and fell into a long silence without saying anything. Then he seriously told him: "It is very important to have deep knowledge. "For this, if necessary, it is necessary to temporarily stop creative activities," he said. After that, Repin began to independently improve his knowledge. He was reading a book incessantly. You admire his will."
This letter is dated February 2, 1965. In Abdulahaq Abdullaev's letter, he gives his advice and life lessons to the young artist studying abroad. Encourages him to learn more, work on himself. Abdulahaq Abdullaev noticed the talent

of the future young artist in time, always asked him how he was doing, and was interested in his living conditions and condition. This can be said to be an example of the teacher-disciple tradition typical of the peoples of the East. The living conditions, inner world, and thoughts of Rozi Choriev at that time are also revealed in these correspondences.

Many people visited Rozi Choriev's workshop. Among them were famous artists, scientists, writers. The artist has always been in creative communication with them. He created their portraits. At that time, articles about Rozi Choriev by well-known people were also published, in which the portrait of the artist expressed through the eyes of the author was described. Among them is the famous singer, People's Artist of Uzbekistan Botir Zokirov's article "Every day is a day of creativity" published in the September 24, 1976 issue of the newspaper "Sovetskaya kultura", which is included in the book. This article can be called a portrait of Rozi Choriev on the path of life and creativity. It tells the story of the author's first meeting with Rozi Choriev, the artist's personality, and his work. Botyr Zokirov describes Rozi Choriev as follows: "...I worked a lot with composers, witnessed the birth of songs. I saw how the directors rehearse and shoot the elephant. I went together with the artists many times to work on etudes. But so far this has not been the case. At that time, I saw a person who devoted himself to art in the form of the artist Choriev. He is an artist who is passionately devoted to creativity, devoted to palette and easel. Yes, he is a strange man! This is because he is always inspired. The artist is always working.

His workshop is not a place within four walls where easels and canvases stand. His workshop is the houses he has visited, the streets he has walked. His workshop is the towns and villages, the people he meets, the landscapes of his continuous travels.

Choriev always draws and writes about everything. He cannot live without it. He cannot stand without drawing and writing."

Articles like this are important sources for fully revealing Rozi Choriev's personality, his artistic world, and his spiritual world.

The third part of the novel-essay is called "The Last Testament of Rozi Choriev". It contains small pictures of the artist's life and creative activity, letters from his personal archive, notes in a notebook, memories and other sources.

Small pictures related to the artist's life are written based on the author's memories. Memories related to the artist are revived in the author's imagination. "Who doesn't know Uzbek?" Rozi Choriev's love and devotion to his native language was shown in the film. We know that the artist grew up in an orphanage and had Russian teachers. The future artist learned the Russian language perfectly here, and later took lessons in Leningrad. According to the tradition of that time, he communicated more in Russian. "Who doesn't know Uzbek?" According to the film, it is shown that in the artist's studio, he played a bet with one of his guests, the artist Bakhtiyor Boboev, about who knows the Uzbek language better. Rozi Choriev, speaking in pure Surkhan dialect, defeated his partner in the bet without saying a single word of Russian. This picture reflects the fact that the artist has not forgotten his mother tongue, his dialect, and his loyalty to his nation, which embodies another human image of him.

In the film called "Among People", the characteristics of Rozi Choriev's character, such as sincerity, openness, and simplicity, are mentioned as follows: "When we stopped at the bread market at the turn of Termiz road near Samarkand, the bread selling girls pushed each other and said, "Here, brother Rozi has come." . Brother Rozi immediately took out his notebook and drew their faces. Even when we stopped at small stations and markets on the steppe or mountain road, people immediately recognized Rozi and greeted him. Some of them were familiar, but most of them were complete strangers. Brother Rozi would open his heart to them, hug them sincerely, ask them something... In fact, everyone was interested in how Brother Rozi could penetrate into the people. With his amazing simplicity and open heart, he attracted people like an iron rod. He looked at people, nature, environment with great love. He did not know how to put himself above someone else, not to brag, the heart of this artist, as innocent as a child, was far from envy, anger, hatred, sarcasm, and sarcasm. That's why the common people sought him out."

Also, in the book "Brother Rozi, bread, restaurant", "Hello sky, hello star, hello man...", "If your wish is sincere...", Rozi Choriev's qualities of generosity, tolerance, humanitarianism and generosity are reflected. . He was not interested in collecting money and wealth. In the books, we can see that he helped his friends and students who needed money, even by selling his paintings. The artist was only interested in creativity, creating new paintings and works. He kept away from luxury and wealth. He lived and created in his poor hut until the end of his life. Greatness was hidden in his modest way of life, in his simplicity, in his devotion to creativity.

In the "Last Testament of Rozi Choriev" section of the novel, the artist's published articles, interviews, statements about his work, letters and correspondence from his personal archive, notes and comments in his side notebook, as well as samples of the author's notes about the artist are presented in the contemporary press. It would not be a mistake to say that they have performed important tasks in the understanding of the figure and phenomenon of Rozi Choriev as a whole.

Here is a note from Rozi Choriev's notebook: "I did not attend my father's funeral." I could not carry my mother's coffin to the cemetery. But I appreciate the value of blood. My dear Uzbek people have appreciated my work, my works have been placed in prestigious museums. I feel the smiles of my good-hearted friends and the gnashing of teeth of envious strangers. I want to share joy with all of you. I am always with you, my dear compatriots.

In these short lines, Rozi Choriev's dreams, regrets, pains, joy and gratitude, sincere heart, and genius words are embodied.

Rozi Choriev introduced Uzbek art to the world, continuing the traditions of Kamoliddin Behzod, a great representative of Eastern painting. His works have taken place in famous museums of the world. Literary scholar Islamjon Yaqubov writes: "The last will and testament of Rozi Choriev" is a novel-essay about such a person whose life and creative destiny were filled with bright colors, beautiful moments, and great successes. At the same time, his life and creative path is characterized by the fact that he is in the grip of dramatic events and authoritarian environment. In fact, the artist Rozi Choriev was a charming person in all respects, and he appeared as a great creative person in the memory of artists, people who knew him, and our people. During his lifetime, the artist literally became a national icon, a symbol of creativity."

Nadir Normatov writes at the end of the novel "Rozy Choriev's last will and testament": "As a conclusion to my stories about Rozy Choriev, I would like to emphasize the following: sometimes the thought crosses my mind: "Didn't she come from another world - from the world of fairy tales?" The reason I say this is, first of all, his passion full of pleasure, his thirst for beauty, and his creativity with inexhaustible enthusiasm. Sometimes looking at him, now he enters like a hare among people who have forgotten what beauty is, and shouts with a flowery voice: "O people! Look how beautiful life is! How beautiful is the art! How beautiful each of you is! Do not forget this! Hurry up, you are not happy for each other! The duty of every artist is to remind people of this fact with his works and his way of life!" it will be like saying" . In this author's characterization, the most important aspects of Rozi Choriev's character are expressed: his love for art and nature, his passion for it.

The book takes the reader into a strange world. The reader lives with the events of the work, has an imaginary conversation with the artist. The novel "Rozy Choriev's last will" describes the entire life of the famous artist in detail. The creation of this work was literally one of the great events in the history of Uzbek literature and art. R. Abdullaev, the chairman of the Union of Composers of Uzbekistan, expressed the following thoughts during the presentation of the book: "This is one of the most valuable works. It helps people to understand and deepen the creativity of Rozi Choriev. No matter if this work falls into the hands of a writer, poet, artist, musician or any other profession, each of them will get some kind of spiritual nourishment from it. Because Nadir Normatov managed to convincingly and impressively describe the life and work of Rozi Choriev, who was an exemplary person for all of us. I think that many such works should be written in the future."

It is known from the history of world literature and art that a number of biographical works have been created on the life and work of famous artists, writers, poets, scientists, political figures, and in general, famous people. There is no doubt that Rozi Choriev is a great artist. He can easily be included among the artists of the world. The life and creative path of a unique artist who devoted his whole life to art and creativity is reflected in a number of works. Nadir Normatov chose a unique composition and style in describing the life and creative path of the great artist. Feeling that the author has a great responsibility, he took a pen in his hand. He was able to demonstrate his artistic and artistic skills in embodying the image of his long-time beloved, confidant friend, a hero who breathed the air of a village - a great artist, the owner of a great heart, and at the same time a simple, humble person.

He artist's ability to use artistic visual tools

Art is a broad concept. It is typical for all art phenomena. Literary critic Hotam Umurov defines artistry as follows: "Artism is a general sign of vivid and impressive depiction of life, a phenomenon that ensures the aliveness, wonder, and impressiveness of the recreated world. That is, artistry includes all elements of artistic creativity (image, character, type, plot, detail, composition, artistic language, means of expression, poetic syntax, genres, style...).

Bahadir Sarimsakov writes about the nature of artistry in his scientific treatise "Basics and Criteria of Artistry": "Artistry is the only common art that reflects reality through re-creative perception in all types of art, based on the unique means and capabilities of these types, and at the same time unites all types of art. is a feature. Art itself does not exist and cannot exist without artistry. Therefore, artistry is the only criterion for all types of art."

Artistry is determined based on several criteria. These criteria are also relative, of course. According to B. Sarimsakov, "Art is a characteristic of a person who knows no boundaries, and its criteria cannot be clearly defined. But the literary-theoretical opinion requires clarifying the most basic criteria of artistry, summarizing the existing artistic experiences in the literary treasury. Therefore, the criteria of artistry cannot be defined completely. Because in connection with the talent of each artist, new aspects and boundaries are discovered. But this does not mean that the criteria of artistry can be defined in general, and that it is useless to try. As the human mind strives to change the laws of nature and society, the psyche and the secrets of the universe within its capabilities, the theory of literature also tries to determine the most general, universal and convincing criteria of the immovable nature called art.

Each work of art is a new world. The artist discovers new aspects of art in his work. One of the most important factors determining the artistic quality is the language of the work. "The skillful use of language elements is important in making the language of a work of art effective. In this regard, writers pay special attention to the effective use of language capabilities. This ensures that each literary work is artistically mature. This in itself determines the skill of using words of each writer, the level of his effective use of each word.

Nadir Normatov is also demanding in the matter of language. The language of literary works is distinguished by the absence of excessive details and lengthy explanations. Sentences are concise and simple. The writer uses more words characteristic of Surkhan dialects. In his works, words and phrases that are disappearing and are preserved in the language of the older generation are common. For example, in the short story "Jaza" in the sentence "The old woman floated to the lake", "piyova" is often used in the language of the inhabitants of the Kohitang highland villages of Surkhandarya, and it means the name of a dish. In the same work, the word "kosapora" in the sentence "If there was no Kosapora, let's take it away" from the Kyrmyz fat language means "she has not yet stepped on the threshold of womanhood." inak" means cow.

In the writer's works, local traditions, customs, traditions, and ceremonies are also widely found. They are important in showing the national color. For example, in the short story "Jazo" the method of treating the mother's stomach in Mergan is given in local conditions: "The old woman put the stone on the gas in the hall and heated it without burning her hands. Then he got up from the bed without leaving his grandson, took off his pants and sat on the stone. ... This is the method of treating the stomach of the sniper momo. First he sits on a hot stone. The stone, especially when heated in the sun, asked for intestinal moisture.

Nadir Normatov's characters effectively use proverbs, proverbs, cursing, sayings, etc. in their speech. For example, "Until you eat meat in a narrow place, shake your fist in a wide place", "Far away horses will neigh, if they are close, they will bite", ("Uncle Ismail's scale"), "He who enters with milk will come out with a soul" ("Punishment"), "If your companion is a dung beetle." , the owner will be dung" ("Zaharmuhra") and the curse "Hoy tilingga kuydurgi chichkur" ("Punishment").

Usually, when someone dies, women and mothers sing aytim (songs of mourning). In the story "Jazo" we encounter the same ceremony at the death of Mom Mergan: "At the gathering of Mom Mergan, who died last week, one day the wife added the same story:
He threw the flax flower,
The star has tears in his eyes,
To our mother like lightning,
Who threw us!
Oh mommy, oh mommy!..

The next day, my nephew,
All faith.
I stabbed him to death,
Four snakes of coral!
Oh mommy, oh mommy!..

It was a curse. There is no greater punishment for a person! Mayram Koshmija saw it with his own eyes: three ghosts slipped out of the women who were mourning and crying. It was that three-sister, three-headed dragon. They could not bear the cruel curse of the people and left the village."

We also come across the saying in the story "Ishmael Father's Scales". It contains a lament sung by his three daughters when Toksonboy the pooch died:

The camel stood up
Chain around his neck.
Don't forget my father,
In the bosom of the black earth.
Say hello when a guest comes,
Say the hotel is empty.
My servant to the guest,
You are a flower, my father.

If I spread the scarf on the loom,
Standing on the fence, he gets wet.
Thinking of the deer, my father,
He stood up and sighed.
My bearded father,
My father's voice is a nightingale."

The narration given by Jonmurad and his father in the story "Zaharmuhra" played an important role in showing the experiences of the heroes of the story and revealing the essence of the work: "Jonmurad looked towards the mountains again. A rustling sound came from the side of the steppe adjacent to the Blue Mountains. Seskandi After all, this is his father's voice. His body trembled and listened:

Did you have a relationship with Mansoor?
It was hard to see someone who had died alive.
My light says, it won't let me go
Did you have a father and I had a son?
Tears fell from Jonmurad's eyes. Involuntarily, the father continued the song:
When I cry, young fat is on my face,
Listen, father, to what I say,
You left, didn't you like this world?
You have a son, and I have?"
Nadir Normatov creates a vivid image of the character by depicting the actions of the characters. For example, "He was thinking about this while shaking the hem of his white scarf" (expressing a thoughtful state) ("Punishment"), "He put one end of his white gauze scarf over his left shoulder and the other side over his right shoulder and gave us a look" (in the sense of showing that he is ready to go somewhere) ("Ishmael Father Scales").

In N. Normatov's historical story "Kamoliddin Behzod", archaic words served as an important descriptive tool in describing the environment of the time in which the great artist lived. For example: "- They said that person, I saw such a scene near Termiz, they are similar. The king asked again that I can see it, but what is its meaning. "My meaning is that people should not become camels. It's like that, our father said. The king said that perhaps the artist Behzad will solve this problem. In any case, I came here to warn you that you should answer this question right away.

It is known that the nickname is actively used in live speech and folklore. Naming people depends on their lineage, profession, physical appearance, character, etc. One of the most important features of Nadir Normatov's work is that the characters of most of his works are nicknamed.

There are various forms of using nicknames in literary works. They can be studied by classifying them as follows:

    1.Nicknames given to people depending on their profession, position, and duties: Vasid Mergan ("On the Mountain"), Bori Muallim ("Panji"), Chori Morboz ("Birds flew from the cliff"), Qabil Lashkar, Orzikul Temirchi ("Bisot") , The next day, Banot the driver, Chori pakhsakash ("Punishment"), Allayor mirob, Chori tuyakash, Damir the butcher, Kholmat the driver ("Uncle Ismail's Scales"), Juma the doctor, Sabir the pigeon, Halima the gambler ("The Two in the Mirror");

    2.Nicknames given to people based on external signs, some physical defects: Ishaq kiishiq ("On the mountain"), Sayficha ("Sayfi brother"), Kar momo ("Deaf mom"), Rajab cholak, Salim tentak ("Birds flew from the cliff"). , Barot kal ("Bisot"), Huri sariq, ("The man under the tree"), Raim kar, Kirmiz semiz, Mayram koshmijja, Bujur kal ("Punishment"), Muhammad tanbal ("Uncle Ismail's Scales"), Ortiq sariq ("Two in the mirror");

3. Nicknames given to people depending on their character: Oykhol bid-bid ("Punishment"), Karim baqiroq ("Bisot"), Musicha kampir (in the sense of being as innocent as a musician) ("Two in the mirror").

In general, in literary works, nicknames served as important factors in showing the characters' character, characteristics, inner and outer appearance.

Epigraphs are also found in the works of N. Normatov. It is known that the writer uses epigraphs in harmony with the spirit of the work to reveal the essence of his work. As an epigraph, folk proverbs, aphorisms, fragments of poems, etc. are often given. In the story "Owner of the Sacred Fish" "A disaster is better than the risk of disaster", in the folk proverb "Two Days of a Life" the poetic line of the Russian poet M. Lermontov "At least a lover for the heart", in the story "The White Shirt of the Moon" "My shirt was white, White although it was odd. The folk song "My heart was attached to another" and in the novel-essay "Rozi Choriev's last will" Jubron Khalil Jubron's thoughts "Art is a step from comprehensible and precise to incredible mystery" and "Remembering is a form of meeting" were chosen as epigraphs. .

Most of the writer's works begin with the content of the message, the image of space and place. In some cases, the reality of the work begins directly from the dialogue. For example, in the story "White Shirt of the Moon" we encounter such a scene:
"- Give me a mulberry...
- It's late. It's morning now.
- No... Now, - Oykuldi caressed, - You will knock now!.."
In addition, the dialogue in the works of the writer served to increase the intensity, tension, and conflict in some dramatic situations. This is evident in the dramatic situation with the three sisters and Mayram in the story "Jaza":
"- Lie! Mayram yelled involuntarily. Look at the speech of pollution. When he strangled the child! Oikhol bid-bid knows very well what happened. He is deliberately slandering that he "strangled his child". - Don't lie, Oyhol bid-bid, - said Mayram, trembling, - shameless!

"Are you delusional now?" Aikhol said with a mocking smile. - If I lied, then why did you give me the carved chest left by your father? Otherwise, why did you leave the yard to me? Is it useless? No! You did this so that no one would know about my secret."

Nadir Normatov expresses reality through the author, narrator-hero. The speech of the narrator-hero usually avoids the traditional method of narration and allows a free, lively approach to the depicted reality. For example, in the story "Uncle Ismail's Scales", this method came in handy in the light, interesting narration of the story being described. It is precisely because the detective spirit prevailed in this story that the speech of the narrator-hero in describing reality played an important role in its more attractive and lively performance. The story begins: "No, I'm not a jeweler. Jewelry scales are actually otameros. If I don't sell it now, it won't happen, bro. Not out of need, no. If not, why am I selling? It has its own history. You come from such a far place as a buyer, well, I'll tell you. Anyway, today you will be our guest...

Two years ago, our sister came home. I was surprised by the message he brought."
While the author describes the reality through the narrator-hero in the story, he reveals the image of the heroes of the work through his eyes. Reality is revealed through his unique tone of speech, opinions, worldview. The language of the story is light, close to the colloquial language.

In the literary works, the inner experiences of the characters are sometimes expressed through an inner monologue. For example, in the novel "Two in the Mirror" the inner experiences of Halima the gambler are described in this way: "But this time it is not motivated. I don't agree with you this time, Malika Khan. The thing is, your mother wants to see me as Black Hair forty years ago.

But years, life has done its job, I am now a completely different person. It's hard to change me now. It's true, since I came to the village, since I saw your mother, I've been in a bad mood. What should I do now, Malika Khan? This is how Halima addressed the gambler Malika in her mind.

In the passage above, Halima the gambler's imaginary address to Malika expresses her inner experiences and thoughts. Halima, who returned from her village after forty years, uses inner monologue to show the situation and thoughts of the gambler.

In conclusion, it should be noted that the effective use of dialects and archaic words of the living colloquial language of the people is one of the most important aspects of Nodir Normatov's work.

GENERAL CONCLUSION

We considered it appropriate to summarize the results of our observations and research conducted in order to determine the artistic skills of Nodir Normatov as follows:

1. Nodir Normatov, a member of the literary generation of the 70s and 80s, was born in the village of Poshkhurd, Surkhan oasis. The writer takes the place where he was born and grew up as a literary place. His heroes are people of this land. The writer's childhood memories and experiences served as literary material. Nadir Normatov usually refers to a topic, event and character that he knows and is close to his heart. Adib mainly writes about the events he witnessed, sometimes participated in, experienced. He is able to draw an exemplary artistic conclusion based on deep logic from seemingly simple events in life. The work of Nadir Normatov has not been sufficiently studied in our literary studies. Although reviews and analytical articles have been published about the writer's works, they cannot fully reveal the essence of the author's work and various aspects of his art. Researching the creative laboratory of Nodir Normatov, his artistic skills from the point of view of today's criteria of interpretation and analysis is one of the urgent issues of our literary studies.

2. "Rural prose" occupies an important place in the work of Nadir Normatov. Even in the first stories of the writer, the Shukshin spirit can be observed. This is especially evident in the stories included in the creator's collection "Kohitang Stories". The main theme of the stories included in this collection is rural life, the joys and sorrows of the people of this land, dreams and aspirations. Nadir Normatov describes the life of the people of Kohitang highland villages, because the writer knows these lands very well, he spent his childhood in these places.

Nadir Normatov's story "Once there was an ant..." was created on the basis of artistic convention. In the story, during the dialogue between the hero of the work and the ant, we encounter the image of human feelings, experiences, and the pain of the times. At the same time, the wide possibilities of realism, richness of layers are evident in the work of the writer. Rare. Although the traditional realistic style is dominant in Normatov's works, polyphonicity, i.e. wide layering, is observed in it. In particular, realistic and non-realistic elements are mixed in some of the writer's works. Nadir Normatov is based on reality, i.e. documentary, in his artistic reflection of the realities of life.

3. Nadir Normatov also created effectively in the short story genre. The stories "Bisot", "Holy Fish Owner", "Punishment", "The Man Under the Tree", "Uncle Ismail's Scales" are not alike in

terms of theme, plot, and style. But it is not difficult to understand that the unique signature of the writer - style, approach to reality is evident in them.

4. The novel "Twins in the Mirror" describes the events related to the life, thoughts, imaginations, dreams, pains and joys, thoughts, experiences and feelings of several characters. Although there are main protagonists in the center of the work, the development of the narrated events is described not only by their activities, but also by the artistic interpretation of the mental state of several characters, what they have seen and experienced, and their memories. The writer's artistic intention is to show the roots of the events that appear simple, but in fact lead to sad and unpleasant consequences and tragedies by describing the complicated and bitter destiny of a person. Several knots and riddles are given in the novel, which will be revealed during the reality of the work. Adib does not open their solution at once. They are led by a detective spirit, a tone.

5. In the writer's prose, the conditional motive is the leading form. When Umar, the hero of the novel "Two in the Mirror", wants to restore Dangana, his wife Malika sets a condition. He says that if he restores the flag, he will leave the house. In general, in the work of Nodir Normatov, the condition-test motive is often found. Uzbek people use the condition-test, which is widely used in fairy tales and epics, as a form of artistic expression. In the story "Owner of the Sacred Fish", Munira makes a condition for her husband Otamurod. He says that he will leave the house if Karim apologizes to the old man. In the story "The Man Under the Tree" Esonboy also has to fulfill certain conditions in order to own the silver nut. Because of these conditions, the heroes of the work are tested.

6. Nadir Normatov's biographical novel "Rozi Choriev's Last Testament" became a novelty in Uzbek literature with its unique composition, style of expression, and form. The author does not follow the path of a dry description of the artist's biography. Reflecting the artist's life from childhood to his death, Adib uses memories, conversations with him and notes in his notebook. The events in the play complement each other. Sometimes the artist's memories, conversations or thoughts are given, sometimes the writer's observations, what he knows, what he witnessed. But they don't get mixed up or confused. The history of creation of the artist's works will not leave the reader indifferent. These are told through the artist's memories and conversations. It is important that "Rozi Choriev's last will" does not bore the reader. A complete portrait of Rozi Choriev is presented in the novel-essay.

7. Nadir Normatov is demanding in language. The language of literary works is distinguished by the absence of excessive details and lengthy explanations. Sentences are concise and simple. The writer uses more words characteristic of Surkhan dialects. In his works, words and phrases that are disappearing and are mostly preserved in the language of the older generation are widely used. In expressing his artistic intention, the writer effectively uses proverbs, proverbs, legends, conventional means, folk colloquial language, dialect and archaic words, which are masterpieces of folk art.

LIST OF REFERENCES USED

1. Normative-legal documents and publications of methodological importance

On the Strategy of Actions for further development of the Republic of Uzbekistan // Xalq sozi, February 8, 2017, No. 28 (6722). - B. 1-2.

2. Mirziyoev Sh. Development of literature and art, culture is a solid foundation for raising the spiritual world of our people // Xalq sozi, August 4, 2017.

3. Mirziyoev Sh. We will build our great future together with our brave and noble people.- Tashkent: "Uzbekistan" NMIU, 2017. - 113 p.

4. Mirziyoev Sh. Critical analysis, strict discipline and personal responsibility should be the daily rule of every leader's activity. Tashkent: Uzbekistan, 2017. – 102 p.

II. Scientific and theoretical literature

5. Literary theory. Two volumes. Volume I (Literary work). - T.: Science, 1978. - 416 p.

6. Literary theory. Two volumes. Volume II (Literary-historical process). - T.: Science, 1979. - 448 p.

7. Literature and time. Articles, literary thoughts, conversations. - T.: Literature and Art, 1981. - 400 p.

8. Aristotle. Poetics. His morals are great. Rhetoric. - T.: New age generation, 2011. - 352 p.

9. Borev Yu. Aesthetics. - 4-e izd., dop. - M.: Politizdat, 1988. - 496 p.

10. Borev Yu. Aesthetics: V 2 t. Smolensk, 1997. T. 1. – 576 s; T. 2. - 640 p.

11. Boltaboev H. Prose and style: A theoretical look at the problem of style and stylistic research in contemporary Uzbek prose. - T.: Science, 1992. - 104 p.

12. Boboev T. Basics of literary studies. Textbook. 2nd edition, revised and supplemented. - T.: Uzbekistan, 2002. - 560 p.

13. Volkov I.F. Theory literature. M., 1995. – 594 p.

14. Vladimirova N. Razvitie Uzbekskoy prose 20th century i voprosy chudojestvennogo perevoda. - T.: Science, 2011. - 336 p.

15. Ginzburg L.O Psychological prose. - L.: The same. l-ra, 1977. – 442 p.

16. Gasparov M.L. Izbrannye trudy. Oh stixax. M., 1997. T.2. - 420 p.

17. Dostmuhammad Kh. The joys of free suffering. - T.: Ma'naviyat, 2000. - 112 p.

18. Esin A.B. Principles and principles of analysis of literary production. - M.: Flinta, Nauka, 2002. - 246 p.

19. Esin A. Literaturovedenie. Culturology: Izbrannye trudy. M., 2003. – 352 p.

20. Dzhorakulov U. Issues of theoretical poetics: Author. Genre. Chronotop. Scientific-theoretical studies, literary-critical articles. - T.: Publishing house named after Gafur Ghulam, 2015. - 356 p.

21. Independence. Literature. Criticism. (Collection). Compiler and preparers for publication: S. Kuronov, R. Haydarova, R. Hakimjonova. - T.: Turon zamin ziya, 2014. - 312 p.

22. Yoldoshev Q. Hot word. - T.: New age generation, 2006. - 548 p.

23. Karim B. The alphabet of the soul. - T.: Publishing house named after Gafur Ghulam, 2016. - 364 p.

24. At the beginning of the big road (literary-critical articles). A collection of articles. - T.: Young Guard, 1987. - 144 p.

25. Uzbek literature of the period of independence. - T.: Publishing house named after Gafur Ghulam, 2006. - 288 p.

26. Mamajonov S. Style polishes. - T.: Literature and Art, 1992. - B.219.

27. Mirzaev I. The magic of art style. - Samarkand, 2000. - B.180.

28. Normatov U. Revolution of the Heart: Articles. - T.: Literature and Art, 1986. - 352 p.

29. Normatov U. Hopeful principles. - T.: Ma'naviyat, 2000. - 112 p.

30. Normatov U. The magic of creation. - T.: Sharq, 2007. - 352 p.

31. Normatov U. Sounds of elegance. - T.: Muharrir, 2010. - 390 p.

32. Life and work of Nadir Normatov in the eyes of contemporaries: articles, reviews, literary conversations. - T.: Publishing house of "San'at" magazine. - 386 p.

33. Normurodov R. Artistic skills of Shukur Kholmirzaev. - T.: "Literary Foundation", 2003. - B.104.

34. Pardaeva Z. Development of artistic aesthetic thinking and Uzbek novelism. - T.: New Generation, 2002. - B.100.
35. Rasulov A. Art is a beautiful novelty: scientific and literary articles, interpretations, etudes. - T.: "Sharq", 2007. - 336 p.
36. Rasulov A. The style is a portrait of talent (Erkin A'zam's work). - T.: New age generation, 2013. - 108 p.
37. Sultan I. Literary theory. Textbook. 2nd edition. - T.: Teacher, 1986. - 408 p.
38. Sarimsakov B. Fundamentals and criteria of art. - T.: Science, 2004. - 128 p.
39. Tyupa V.I. Khudojestvennyy discourse (Vvedenie v teoriyu literatury). Tver, 2002. – 80 p.
40. Toychiev U. Criteria of artistry in Uzbek literature and their virtues. - T.: New age generation, 2011. - 508 p.

41. Toraev D. Gloss of colorful images: literary-critical articles. - T.: Akademnashr, 2014. - 200 p.
42. Tolaganova S. Morphology of the work of art. - T.: Turon zamin ziya, 2016. - 176 p.
43. Umurov H. Literary theory. - T.: "Sharq", 2004. - 256 p.
44. Ulug'ov A. Edges of our short story. Monograph. – T.: Read

III. Collections, articles in newspapers and magazines

1. Akramov G'. Artistic word and theoretical thought // UzAS. - September 6, 1985.
2. Vladimirova N. Researches in novel writing // Uzbek language and literature. – 1988. – No. 6. - B.13-16.
3. Isomiddinov Z. Two women / Uzbek literary criticism (anthology). - T.: TURON-IQBOL, 2011. - B. 372-385.

4. Yoldoshev Q. Sincere image temperature // Language and literature education. – 2010. – No. 7. - B. 42-54.

5. Roots of spiritual crisis. Roundtable discussion // Youth. – 1989. – No. 3. - B. 66-72.

6. Normatov N. Creative freedom and new principles // UzAS. – November 26, 2010'.

7. Normatov N. In the breadth of the heart // UzAS. - September 24, 2010.

8. Normatov N. With new signature // UzAS. - October 8, 2010.

9. Normatov N. Conclusions born from comparisons // UzAS. - May 20, 2011.

10. Normatov N. I fed the water... it took away my thoughts...// UzAS. - February 11, 2011.

11. Normatov U. Small miracles // UzAS. - May 14, 1982.

12. Normatov U. Realism in action // UzAS. - July 22, 1983.

13. Nazarov B. On some methodological issues of the study of literary influence and typological closeness / Uzbek literature. Influence and typology (Proceedings of the scientific-theoretical conference of the Republic). - T.: "Muharrir", 2013. - B. 6-16.

14. Otaev R. Human fate in the story / At the beginning of the big road (literary-critical articles). - Tashkent: Young Guard, 1987. - B. 57-68.

15. Ulug'ov A. Wish to Nasser // UzAS. - March 17, 1989.

16. Khudoyberganov N. Is the description enough? Youth prose: research, results, difficulties // UzAS. - September 27, 1985.

17. Khudoyberganov N. Modernity and skill (round bell) / Star of the East. – 1985. – No. 6. - B. 161-163.

18. Khudoyberganov N. Both himself and his words / I think of you, contemporary (thoughts,

reflections, discussions about Uzbek prose, poetry and literary criticism of the 70s and 80s). - T.: Literature and Art, 1983. - B. 90-130.

IV. Dissertation and abstracts

19. Dostmuhammedov Kh. Renewal of artistic thinking in contemporary Uzbek storytelling (on the example of stories from the second half of the 80s and the beginning of the 90s): dissertation written for the degree of Ph.D. - Tashkent, 1995. - 149 p.

20. Davronova Sh. Literary process and writer's creative individuality: dissertation written for the degree of candidate of sciences in philology. - Tashkent, 2004. - 163 p.

21. Imamkarimova M.M. The interpretation of national values in the works of O'tkir Hoshimov: the abstract of the dissertation written for the degree of candidate of philological sciences. - Tashkent, 2001. - 22 p.

22. Nurmatov A. Polyphonism in a work of art: thesis abstract written for the degree of candidate of sciences in philology. - Tashkent, 1996. - 24 p.

23. Pirnazarova M. Methodological research in modern Uzbek novels: dissertation written for the degree of Ph.D. - Tashkent, 2006. - 151 p.

24. Radjapova F. Style and poetic language in Uzbek short stories of the period of independence: Doctor of Philosophy (PhD) dissertation on philology. - Tashkent, 2018. - 52 p.

25. Sattorova G. The problem of national character in Uzbek storytelling of the 1990s (on the example of the stories of G. Hotam, H. Dostmuhammad, N. Eshonqul): dissertation written for the degree of candidate of philological sciences. - Tashkent, 2002. - 135 p.

26. Sopieva Sh. Khairiddin Sultan's story-writing skills: dissertation written for the degree of Ph.D. in Philology. - Tashkent, 2006. - 160 p.

27. Kholmurodov Abduhamid. Uzbek short story: problems of development (last quarter of the 20th century): Dissertation written for the degree of doctor of philological sciences. - Tashkent, 2008. - 291 p.

28. Shofiev Obidjon. Erkin A'zam's prose art (irony and image): Doctor of Philosophy (PhD) dissertation on philological sciences. - Samarkand, 2019. - 50 p.

. Hamidova M. The problem of the national hero in modern Uzbek literature: dissertation abstract written for the degree of candidate of sciences in philology. - Tashkent, 2001. - 24 p.

88. Hamraev K. Poetics of composition in contemporary Uzbek narrative: Doctor of Philosophy (PhD) dissertation in philological sciences. - Tashkent, 2018. - 52 p.

V. Literary and artistic publications

1. Azam E. Farewell to a fairy tale: short stories and stories. - T.: National Encyclopedia of Uzbekistan, 2007. - 200 p.
2. Normatov N. Read the stories. - T.: Literature and Art, 1977.
3. Normatov N. Birds flew from the cliff. Stories. - T.: Literature and Art, 1986.
4. Normatov N. The house where the rainbow lives. A documentary story. - T.: Yulduzcha, 1990.
5. Normatov N. Golubye nut. Narrator and artist. - T.: Young Guard, 1990.
6. Normatov N. Barely. - T.: Kamalak, 1991.
7. Normatov N. Rozi Choriev's last will. - T.: "San'at", 2008. - 264 p.
8. Normatov N. Bisot: stories, stories. - T.: "Sharq", 2012. - 448 p.
9. Normatov N. Twins in the mirror. - T.: "Uzbekistan", 2013. - 320 p.

10. Shukshin V. The old man, the girl and the sun: Stories / translated by O'tkir Hoshimov and Khairiddin Sultanov. - T.: Literature and Art, 1980. - 176 p.

Internet sites:

1. http://ziyonet.uz
2. http: //kitob.uz
3. http://tas–ix.tafakkur.net
4. http://kh-davron.uz
5. http://ziyouz.uz

TABLE OF CONTENTS

INTRODUCTION

The nature of images in the novel "Two in the mirror"

The artistic expression of the hero's experiences in the novel "Rozy Choriev's last will"

....

The artist's ability to use artistic visual tools...

GENERAL CONCLUSION

LIST OF REFERENCES USED

www.ingramcontent.com/pod-product-compliance
Lightning Source LLC
LaVergne TN
LVHW010343070526
838199LV00065B/5784